HOW DO YOU RECOVER AFTER
A LOST RELATIONSHIP?

ANGUS NELSON

LOVE'S COMPASS

How Do You Recover After a Lost Relationship?

Copyright © 2010 Angus Nelson

Scripture quotations marked MSG are taken from *The Message*, copyright © by Eugene H. Peterson. Published by Nav Press, Colorado Springs, Colorado, in association with Alive Communications, Colorado Springs, Colorado.

Scripture quotations marked NKJV are taken from the *Holy Bible*, New King James Version. Copyright © 1982. Used by permission of Thomas Nelson, Inc., Nashville, Tennessee.

*I dedicate this book to my lovely wife, Samantha.
Thank you for the inspiration and encouragement
you never seem to exhaust. May our children be
inspired by the love and laughter we share.
My fondest affections, baby!*

ACKNOWLEDGEMENTS

First and foremost, I want to thank my parents. I thank you for your incredible patience and relentless encouragement, even through my darkest days. To my wife, Samantha, this book would not be here without your insistence—you understood that this story brought you the man that I am so that I could be humbled by the woman that you are. To my daughters Sydney and Scarlett, may you discover the power of grace and the wisdom not to learn lessons the hard way. To Evan, you're not bad for a Canadian.

Finally, to the men that stood by my side, cried tears when appropriate, and slapped my head when necessary: Norm Moeller, Don Schneider, Glenn Burt, Patrick "Dale" Klaybor, Ron Marquardt, Clint Byars, Walter Strankman, Rusty Nelson, and most of all, but by far not least, Bruce Martin: Thank you for believing in me when at times I didn't believe in myself.

FOREWORD

On the following pages, you'll read the story of my husband, the self-proclaimed manwhore. I'm sure people will wonder how I feel reading a story as raw and honest as Angus's. As always, when it comes to Angus, I am amazed at his ability to share truth so boldly. Funny enough, this is one of the things that drew me to him when we first met. I think it is a characteristic that many wish they possessed, myself included, but lack the courage it takes to do so… which is why I would never be able to lay out my story so openly for all the world to read!

I must say, I am intensely grateful for the story you are about to read, while at the same time incredibly saddened. Grateful, because it is a story that ultimately brought he and I together, a journey that makes Angus the man he is today. For that reason, how could I begrudge that? Saddened, because I wish there was another way for him to have learned the lessons that so powerfully shaped him into the man with whom I fell so madly in love.

His story is particularly heartbreaking at times. One always hopes that the people one loves never has to endure tragedy or difficult times in life, and one especially hopes that those hardships are never brought about as a direct result of their poor life choices.

As the wife of this man, who experienced great pain in his search to find love and be loved, a man whose heart and spirit were broken during his many failed attempts to fill a void deep within himself, I did not have the benefit of saving him from those disasters in life. Rather, I can only hope one thing for him now: that he would learn from and never repeat the story you are about to read.

We share this with you today with no regret, and for one reason: we are sure it will touch you. We hope you will read this story and be able to relate to it in some way, to see yourself in the story of a man, lost and searching for love. This is a tale of a heart given away too quickly and without thought, of derailed relationships, and of the baggage that often accompanies that.

In a time when saving one's self for a singular soul mate is the minority experience, we all have lived this man's story in some small way, though perhaps not to its full extent. And if there is a way to learn from him, before experiencing the heartbreak yourself, then this story was not shared in vain.

SAMANTHA NELSON
April 2009

TABLE OF CONTENTS

	Acknowledgments	v
	Foreword	vii
	Introduction	1
ONE	*The Need to Feel Loved*	7
TWO	*Into the Fire*	14
THREE	*On the Brink*	25
FOUR	*Freefall*	30
FIVE	*Post-Splat!*	44
SIX	*Spiritual Schizophrenia*	53
SEVEN	*The Things We Tell Ourselves*	62
EIGHT	*Open Heart Surgery*	71
NINE	*Fighting the Instinct*	83
TEN	*Control Freak*	92
ELEVEN	*Reconnaissance*	100
TWELVE	*Taking the Plunge*	108
THIRTEEN	*Celebrations*	117
FOURTEEN	*The Compass*	126
	The Last Word	139

INTRODUCTION

I used to hate Valentine's Day. If you're out there and single, chances are you hate it, too. On the surface, it's a celebration of romance, but that's nothing more than a party line.

If you're not in a relationship, and have no prospects for being in one, it is one of the most depressing days of the year. A celebration of romance is the perfect opportunity for people to feel bad about themselves for not having any. Though this kind of misery goes against the spirit of the holiday, it's a natural byproduct.

Hollywood certainly hasn't helped matters. Hollywood loves Valentine's Day. In the context of a film, everybody can have a happy ending. The possibilities intrinsic to a blank piece of paper in a writer's typewriter are endless. If a character is lonely, the solution is obvious: write in a love interest, custom-made for the situation at hand. If only life was this fortuitous! Most of us can attest to the fact that it is not. Those who are unlucky in love don't magically experience reversals of fortune overnight.

There have been moments in my life when I felt the urge to shake my fists up at the heavens and scream, "Who's writing this thing anyway?" At times, my life has been a complete train wreck. Though I'll fill in the details in the pages that follow, for the moment you can take my word for it. When it comes to love, I've been to hell and back, and back into hell.

Love...

Even to ask the question "What is love?" is cliché. But let's pretend we're in Hollywood for a moment, where there's no cliché too trite or silly not to be revisited over and over again. Yup, you guessed it. That's another thing Hollywood loves: clichés. Seriously, if somebody completely ignorant on the subject decided to take a crash course on love from popular cinema, they'd be in for a rough ride in the real world. The sad thing is that a lot of people learn this way.

If your expectations of eternal bliss are lifted straight from the climactic scenes of *The Notebook*, you're headed for some massive disappointments. But that kiss was amazing, wasn't it? I don't know about you, but every kiss I've ever shared with my wife has been at least that spectacular, if not better. Every time it rains, we run off to the nearest beach to make out... Oh man, if only that were true.

Here are a few of Hollywood's most memorable lessons:

1. Every dramatic relational breakup will include walking or apologizing in the rain (*Say Anything*).
2. You may have already been with Mr. or Ms. Right the whole time, but just didn't realize it (*When Harry Met Sally*).
3. You can find true love in thirty seconds just by laying eyes on the "Perfect One," trumping any pre-

vious relationship, even one you're currently in. All it takes is a single, passing glance (*Sleepless in Seattle*).

4. Love is strong enough to change someone (*Jerry McGuire, As Good As It Gets, Reality Bites,* ad nauseum).

5. Despite the fact that all your friends have told you that this person is completely not right for you, you decide that you're not a snob like them. You know that this love is the real thing (*Titanic, Pretty Woman,* and *Sweet Home Alabama*).

Don't think these are the only ones, either. I could write an entire book on Hollywood's erroneous love connections. A quick glance at movies like *Casablanca, Gone With the Wind, The Way We Were,* or *An Affair to Remember* would stand testament to that. Let it be simply said that if you're treating the movie theater like an advice column, you're barking up the wrong tree.

Of course, every once in a while the movies get it right. There's a scene in *Babel* that really choked me up when I saw it for the first time. Fine, I'll admit it, I cried the second and third times, too. I'm a sentimental guy. Sit me down with a chick flick and make sure to keep the Kleenex coming.

One of the movie's storylines involves a married couple that decides to visit Morocco in a bid to save their floundering relationship. Having just come through the trauma of losing a child, the pair has a lot of repair work to do. They were stone cold with each other, and it didn't look like they were making much progress, when a stray bullet passed through the window of their tour bus, striking the woman in the shoulder. They're in such a remote area that it's impossible to get to a hospital. In fact, the bus just leaves them behind in a small village where they end of fending for themselves.

In the scene I'm talking about, one of the most powerful, intense film moments I've ever seen, the man cradles his wife in his arms. As he assures her that she isn't going to die, you can see his face is full of uncertainty. Crying, she admits to him that, unable to hold it in, she's peed herself. She's in unbelievable pain, but in this moment, amidst tears and inappropriate laughter, they share a degree of intimacy so raw and so resonating that they're able to reconnect with in a real way

It's not warm and fuzzy. It's not Valentine's Day.

It's reality.

This is the kind of love that awaits you, and there's nothing silly or trite about it.

The desire of my heart is that you, those who have been broken and hurt by a relationship, would find hope. There is no situation that can't be redeemed, no hurt that cannot be healed, and no circumstance that determines your demise.

Wherever you are in your story, we want you to experience your own Hollywood ending. We all want to see the good guy win and the underdog beat the odds. May you be assured that, even during your darkest hours, forgiveness and restoration are available to you.

The man you're about to read about is a stranger
to me now. He died long enough ago to escape my
recollection, yet there's no running from the lessons
he taught me. In the pages that follow, I hope
you learn as much from him as I...

CHAPTER ONE
The Need to Feel Loved

I slid my forefinger over the bottle of Budweiser, my free hand resting on the bar. The calluses from years of guitar playing kept catching on the label. I didn't mind; in fact, it was my only source of entertainment. My mouth was awkwardly wrapped around a bummed cigarette. It was the kind I hated, a Marlboro Light, which always tasted stale in my mouth, but it was all I could negotiate after exhausting my usual brand, Camel Turkish Gold.

As my eyes drifted across the smoky pub where I'd spent so many late nights singing karaoke, I found a number of familiar faces looking back at me through the haze. The regular crowd was milling about, just like any other small town bar in America. Normally I would have made conversation, but tonight things were different. Peculiar even. My emotions were about as gloomy as country music at Christmas time. Nonetheless, I was aware of everything, my ears picking up the essentials of each discussion going on around me. Every interaction, every motion caught my attention. I wasn't ordinarily so astute, so tuned in to my surroundings, but like I said, it was a peculiar night.

Melissa sat on the stool next to me, cradling a drink of her own. I debated whether or not to tell her what was going on, to unleash my inner pain. It wasn't going to be pretty, and yet I thought she might lend a sympathetic ear, having been separated from her second husband for several months. Her own situation made a small, pathetic part of me feel a bit better. True, I was on the brink of divorce, but at least it was still my first marriage. Fortunately, the arrogant thought vanished almost as quickly as it occurred to me.

Sensing my internal conflict, she asked me if there was anything wrong. Stupid instinct kicking in, I lied. Why did I always do that? I was overwhelmed with regret the moment the words came out of my mouth. Perhaps I wanted to protect myself and preserve whatever dignity I still felt, to dismiss her offer of help. Maybe I could pretend everything was fine just a little bit longer, just long enough for a miracle to occur. But nothing about my situation was fine. How had everything gone so horribly, horribly wrong? I wanted to scream, to curl up in the fetal position, to collapse into a heap on the floor... A voice in the back of my mind reminded me that no display of hysterics would magically do away with the years of unacknowledged hurt that had built up in my heart like bad cholesterol.

Our conversation that night had started off innocently enough. Melissa's family had helped me out with a non-profit I was running, so in theory we had a lot to talk about. We joked, engaged in some harmless flirtation, I forced laughter, and she saw right through me. Looking back, it seems obvious that she would easily penetrate my thinly veiled deception. I've never been any good at reining in my emotions. Truthfully, nobody in the bar needed to ask what kind of mood I was in; I was wearing my anguish on my sleeve. For one thing, I was uncommonly reserved, hardly saying a word, which is the first sign of trouble for anyone who really knows me—like Melissa did. I was subconsciously hanging my head and there was a strange slump to my posture.

There was no fooling her, so she asked again. Was there anything wrong? Was there anything I needed to talk about? Inside, I was screaming a full-throated, Yes! Outwardly, I said nothing, holding my façade in place just a little longer, perhaps still hoping for that miracle. Then, after another pregnant pause, I caved. I spilled my story, revealing the ugly truth that my marriage of two years was over.

I felt like such a failure. The impossibility of my situation still hadn't entirely sunk in. I was dazed and confused, like a deer caught in headlights.

Only a few nights before, my wife had come over to the house to discuss the division of property. Division of property? Just as marriages aren't designed to be temporary, there are certain things that just can't be conveniently split in two. My wife and I had built a life together! It was one of the most difficult two hours of my life, an evening of such deep pain, regret, and sorrow that I knew I would never forget it. I didn't even know if I would be able to make it to the next week. And yet there we were, dividing up everything we owned like we were picking teams for kickball. The biggest items got snatched up first, then we whittled down through articles increasingly insignificant until every last thing was spoken for. We bartered endlessly until a line was determined as "half."

During the negotiations, the phone rang. I sat idly by as my wife whimsically frolicked her way through a chat with the man I had walked in on her making out with. Her tone reminded me of a 16-year-old schoolgirl admitting to another girl that she had a crush on a boy. My stomach was nauseous, heaving, my breath labored, my hands sweaty, shaking uncontrollably. It took everything in me to force back the anxiety attack I knew was just around the corner. After ten minutes of absolute nonsense, I interrupted the conversation. Through dry vocal cords, I asked her whether or not she wanted to finish up this ordeal. She hesitated, then quickly said goodbye. I sat motionless as she set the cell phone down on the table.

Now that we were free to continue, I found myself struggling to draw breath. Have you ever been in so much emotional pain that you feared any sudden movement would literally cause you to crumble to the ground? That's exactly how I felt. My eyes were glazed, my heart raced, and the humiliation and mockery of my situation bore down on me like a ton of cement. I felt my face go flush and I itched all over—the analytical part of my brain informed me that this was because my blood was purging toxins from my body. Whatever the reason, I was too immobilized to scratch the itch. In some ways, I felt like I was in shock.

Though I know I made it through the experience, I don't actually remember what happened next. My mind clouded over at that point, sparing me from having to relive the remainder of the division of assets over and over for the rest of my life. I'm almost certain the sheer overload of excruciating agony repressed my memories of the hour that followed.

What happened after that hour, however, I remember vividly. Like it was yesterday, unfortunately.

My wife collected up her legal pad, now scribbled from top to bottom with notes and agreements about who got what. She slipped her purse over her shoulder and picked up the now-cooled caramel macchiato still languishing in her favorite, holiday-red coffee cup. Avoiding the awkward, drawn-out goodbye I both desperately needed and very much wanted to steer clear of, she proceeded toward the front door.

But she didn't quite get that far. In the span of a single second, she stopping suddenly in the middle of the living room and turned. What she was about to do was so bizarre I couldn't have expected it. After a short pause in which our eyes found and locked onto each other, she asked if she "could at least have a hug."

The request caught me flatfooted. It was a moment I had longed for countless times since our separation eight months before. Caught off-guard, I obliged.

I arose from the couch I was slumped in. The moment my arms went around her, she melted into me. Her walls came down, an inevitability we had both been fighting since seeing each other that day. She cried and cried into the front of my shirt, soaking it through as she lamented, "I don't want to get divorced! I can't do it all over again. I don't know what to do."

Although I couldn't bring myself to cry with her, I continued to hold her for several long minutes. I remember telling her that I understood what she was going through and that I would be there for her no matter what her decision was. We stood together for quite some time. After a while, we dropped ourselves onto the couch and she leaned back into my chest, where I just held her and ran my fingers through her hair, a simple pleasure I would never again have the chance to repeat. It was a surreal moment.

It was a glimmer of hope that was immediately snuffed out.

Her cell phone rang and she pulled away to answer it. It was my soon to be former father-in-law calling to check in. Though I never found out what the call was about, all I know was that this final moment of intimacy between us was lost. Whatever heat had been exchanged in that long embrace had been completely extinguished by the cold splash of water that was her ring tone.

As I unraveled my tale of marital woe, Melissa did the best thing she could have done: she simply listened, not offering a word of advice. I'm grateful she didn't respond with her own break-up stories—she had more than a few—since all I was looking for was a shoulder to cry on. In my exhausted, emotionally-depleted state, she was the perfect friend in the most imperfect situation of my life.

Before leaving, she put a hand on my shoulder and spoke for the romantic in all of us. "She's never going to go through with it," she told me.

"We'll see," I murmured, my eyes glancing at my watch. It was after midnight now. The two of us shared one last smile before she walked away, stepping out the doors and disappearing into the cold winter night.

I reached down the bar and picked up my now-empty beer bottle, once again skimming my finger over its surface, tracing the raised edges of the Budweiser logo. I went back into observer mode. With almost supernatural powers, I felt as though I could discern every motive of every interaction between the other patrons that night. After a few minutes of scanning the crowd, I came to one simple conclusion: no one wanted to be alone. I saw person after person trying to work their mojo, their magic, on members of the opposite sex, to mixed results. It's a picture to be repeated every night in every pub around the world.

The lyrics to the Blues Brothers' song "Everybody Needs Somebody to Love" ran through my mind until I wondered how long it would be before I could get the tune back out. As I re-hearsed the chorus in my head, I realized what was wrong with it. It wasn't so much that everybody needed someone to love as they needed to feel loved.

That night, I needed to feel loved.

CHAPTER TWO
Into the Fire

I got married for the first time at the age of 30. Considering that the national average is somewhere in the ballpark of 27, I was just slightly behind the 8-ball. I had sex three times prior to that, all before I was 17. My longest romantic relationship before marriage lasted a mere two months. Sad to say, by modern-day standards these numbers practically qualify me for monk status.

I had one other relationship with an Irish girl that could be described as serious, but it was conducted entirely over long distance and the two of us never shared so much as a goodnight kiss. We were "together" for a year and a half. We talked every Sunday night on the phone for countless hours. Truthfully, we had very similar plans for our lives. And in case you're wondering, yeah, it's true; she had a wicked cool accent.

Unfortunately, while we were getting to know each other, she was at school in Santa Barbara, California, and I may as well have been on the other side of the planet: Central Wisconsin.

Trying to make it work between us was more challenge than I was up for.

I mentioned that I was running a non-profit organization at the time of my divorce, but this story finds its start at the tail end of what had been a successful youth outreach program. Over two years, 15,000 young people took part in events at RockWater, which I founded with my brother. Admittedly, it was poorly managed at times and terribly under budget, but we accomplished a lot of good in our small town. RockWater was a safe haven for teens and young adults in Wausau, Wisconsin.

In late 2000, one of my volunteers was a young woman I had just started getting to know. She was one of the most beautiful women I had ever met and, even though I was over a year into my long-distance relationship, I was curious. Of course, I wasn't going to cheat on my existing girlfriend, so I decided to call her up and find out where she stood with our relationship. Being so far away, it didn't seem to be going anywhere. When I posed the question, what I really wanted to hear was, "I'm in it. Let's wait and be patient. I'm totally into you." Instead, her answer was, "Well, I've still got two years of school ahead of me. I don't know where you or I'll be at that time."

In response, I told her about the girl I had met and that I felt it was time to end things. Frustratingly, I later realized that what my girlfriend had wanted me to say was, "I'm in it. Let's wait and be patient. I'm totally into you." Isn't it interesting how we don't always say what we really want to? Considering where that decision took me, I deeply regret breaking up with that Irish girl.

So I left the pure and slow-forming relationship in order to pursue this new pretty face that had walked into my life. As a student of pop culture, and film in particular, that's what I was supposed to do. Right? After all, I'm sure it was modeled to me in a Hollywood movie at some point.

Being so shy on romantic experience, I was totally unprepared for the world I was about to step into. The woman I thought I was getting involved with turned out to be someone completely different. Ironically, I was someone different, too, and didn't know it. My impression of her from the time she had volunteered at RockWater was that she was quiet and reserved. This was the polar opposite of me, and perhaps because of this I was immediately intrigued.

The more I got to know her, the more I found out about her personal struggles too. There were a lot of them. Her past was littered with the roadkill of sexual flings and broken relationships. I brushed past what should have been warning signs without really taking them into consideration. As far as I was concerned, the past would stay in the past. How naïve I was to think that our relationship would be immune to the pitfalls that had sabotaged all the others in her life.

Mind you, I was hardly the picture of perfection myself. I can't place the blame for all the dysfunction that was to come solely on her shoulders. To do so would be both unfair and irresponsible. Through several late night conversations, I shared with her my insecurities, inner loneliness, and early years of sexual experimentation. I loved being able to tell her anything, to be able to reveal things about myself I had never talked about openly. After such a long period of wondering if I would ever find someone to be with, here was a woman who I felt I could finally be myself around. It was an intoxicating, almost addictive experience.

Little did I know, I was already speeding down the road to divorce. It seems inevitable in retrospect; it was a low probability marriage right from the start. You see, the average person trudging through the snowstorm that is the dating scene in America has already experienced the emotional equivalent of four divorces. Don't believe me? Let's admit it. Most of us live self-destructively. If you're anything like me, at some point you gave yourself away at the drop of a hat just to avoid feeling lonely one more day, one more hour, one more minute. I'm not just talking about giving yourself away sexually, though that's a huge part of it, because sex comes with baggage ... far more than you may realize. We also give ourselves away emotionally to anyone who's available, mostly to people who have the same self-esteem deficiencies we have. That's because people who have lost value for themselves tend to attract other people who have lost value for themselves.

In America today, almost all of us are value-starved. We don't know who we are, where we come from, or why we should even care. Unfortunately, this confusion translates into pain, rejection, and isolation, similar to what is experienced when one goes through divorce. Most people have been through this cycle many times over.

You don't need to have actually been legally married to know what I'm talking about. Emotional marriage has the same effect, and for that you don't even need a ceremony. Emotional marriage happens when we're not paying attention: while in close working environments, sharing common interests, or of course, engaging in sexual activity. The bond that forms gives us the twittery, butterflies-in-the-stomach feeling we mistakenly identify as "falling in love." You see, love isn't something that happens to us just because; it isn't something we fall into without our consent. Love occurs when we choose it. Unfortunately, most of us—myself included—are guilty of falling for someone by default, thinking we don't have a choice in the matter.

How wrong we are.

You see, my future wife and I both "needed" someone. I needed her to complete me, to be the source of my self-worth. She made me feel loved, whole, and significant… needs that I should never have been looking to another human being to fulfill. Just as much as I needed her, she needed me and the attention I gave her. Like everyone, she craved love and significance, and the more intimate our sharing sessions became, the more she began to see me as a way to fill that void.

It wasn't long before we moved beyond late night conversations into the realm of dating. At the beginning, everything was wonderful. At the risk of repeating a cliché, everything about my world seemed brighter. I was brimming with confidence and excitement. At last, I had arrived! I was in a relationship that was going somewhere.

But even at that early juncture, trouble was already just around the corner. After only a few weeks of dating, she came into my office at RockWater, crying uncontrollably. The nurturing part of my personality, my love for people, charged into the situation at full gallop. Whatever was wrong with my girl, I was going to fix it. I thought I was prepared to handle whatever crisis was over the horizon.

How wrong I was about that.

I sat with her for the next few minutes, doing everything I could to keep my mouth from dropping open in astonishment as she explained her dilemma.

She was pregnant.

I couldn't believe what I was hearing. After all, we had never had sex. For this, she had an explanation: On the night of her birthday, just a few short weeks before we started seeing each other, she went to a pub to meet a guy friend of hers and ended up spending the night with him. It was an indiscretion she had come to regret almost immediately. Now that she was with child, she knew this guy wasn't an ideal candidate for becoming a husband and father. She was scared, humiliated, and worst of all alone.

But now I was caught in the middle of an impossible situation. When I initially wanted to "fix" her problem, how could I have known the magnitude of what I was getting myself into? Ultimately, I decided to be the hero, the knight in shining armor to rush to her rescue. In truth, this crisis played directly into my already well-developed savior complex. She needed me more than ever now! I could be the guy she depended on in her deepest, darkest desperation.

So I chose to step up and father this child. A few weeks later, I proposed.

From the beginning, our relationship was based on needy, desperate human behavior. We were both emotionally and spiritually immature, and we didn't have the time to develop ourselves as a couple the way we would have if her expanding baby bump hadn't been such an overwhelming factor in the timing of our nuptials. We had met in September, started dating in October, and were engaged by Christmas. We quickly set the date of our shotgun wedding, April 14, 2001, giving ourselves three and a half months to work out the details of both our special day and our ensuing lives together.

Before we made it to the altar, however, she miscarried. It seems obvious in hindsight that we should have postponed the wedding and taken the time we needed to either cement our relationship or discover that it wasn't meant to be. I can't tell you how badly I wish we had taken that time. Some solid couples counseling, at least six months' worth, could have gone a long way. But our preparations and pride had become more important. By this time, so many of the arrangements were in place that we decided not to reschedule. The wedding went ahead as planned.

I should have listened to my dad. Evidently, he had been paying better attention to my situation than I was. He privately questioned our relationship and widely observed that my soon-to-be wife's melancholy personality might not complement my own. My dad is a man of few words, but he felt my coming marriage an important enough development to say something. I didn't listen.

It's a huge mistake not to listen to those around you. When you are confronted with these kinds of seemingly critical discussions, you're going to come into contact with hard questions about the person you are with. Don't shy away from it. Make yourself face these hard questions! With the help of friends and family, be honest about whether or not you really have the chemistry you need with this person to go the distance. Romantic feelings can be extremely deceptive, and even pathological. Your first impression may not, in fact, be "true love."

Again, this is something I had to learn the hard way. As I teetered on the brink of marriage, I discounted and ignored most of the advice I was getting from people in my life who were very close to me. Instead of embracing what they had to say and choosing to face it head-on, I isolated myself and ended up paying a heavy price. We've all heard that marriage commitments are long-term. We know this intellectually, but I'm not sure any of us who haven't yet experienced marriage truly know what it means. It's no-turning-back *forever*. You owe it to yourself to take into account the input of those you respect, and who respect you back.

The wedding itself was simple and elegant. We rented the ballroom of a local social club and filled it with flowers. Classy jazz and a spectacularly sunny Wisconsin spring made it a day to remember. I greeted my father-in-law to be with a kiss on the cheek, surprised my bride with a solo vocal performance, and maintained my typically humorous disposition throughout. We couldn't afford a lavish honeymoon, so we settled for a two-night stay at a hotel thirty minutes from home.

As a newlywed who had (mostly) saved himself for marriage, I had a number of false expectations and hopes for the interactions we would have in the bedroom. For instance, I had read and heard that the national average for sex among married couples was two to three times a week. Thank you, Hollywood, once again. Apparently, I had gotten all excited for nothing; if we had sex two to three times a month, it was a good month.

As inexperienced as I was in the, er… intimate arena, I knew this was not normal. I was having to wait up to three weeks between coitus, and it messed me up, playing into my growing insecurities. I came to view myself as undesirable and unattractive. I was absolutely humiliated by our inability to connect in the bedroom.

I knew my wife had been with other men before I came along, so it seemed to me that she had perhaps used sex as a means of getting into and maintaining her former relationships. Now that we were bound under a contract of marriage, she might not have felt like she had to debase herself for my benefit. In my mind, I convinced myself that she didn't make sex a priority. Sex for me, and for most men I imagine, is a connection point for intimacy. I began to feel disconnected and taken for granted.

Matters were made worse by the fact that I lacked the emotional maturity necessary to communicate what I wanted or needed. I would pout, argue, and throw tantrums to get my way. When sex wasn't happening in our relationship, I responded by vocally complaining about it. Given my wife's nature, this was the worst possible way I could have expressed my feelings. She longed for safety and understanding, whereas I simply wanted to proclaim my dissatisfaction. The result was that the more I ranted, the more my wife came to resent me.

The simple truth is, I didn't know how to deal with conflict. I was completely ineffective, and it is an area in which I have grown considerably since. As a result, the subject of conflict resolution is close to my heart. You see, every relationship must include some form of conflict from time to time. It's a healthy and necessary reality. Sadly, the fact is that some people just don't fight nicely, let alone fight fair. They'll use whatever weapon or leverage they can get their hands on, regardless of what it will do to the other person emotionally.

Sarcasm, condescending tones, silent treatments, door slamming, extensive yelling, getting hung up on, holes punched in sheetrock, or even sudden disappearances demonstrate huge, HUGE red flags… not that I know anything about these demonstrations. I'm just saying.

I really think every one of us deserves to be treated with a reasonable amount of value, honor, and respect—and yet my wife and I couldn't have been more disrespectful to each other. When we fought, we treated each other like garbage. Unfortunately, what I believed intellectually, that everyone deserves to be treated with value, I could not manifest with a self-worth so bruised.

Sex was only one area in which I felt inadequate. I took everything personally. My wife was exhausted much of the time from pushing through school and work, fraying her already fragile state of mind. When I added to that the pressure to perform in the bedroom, I was only making the situation worse. Much, much worse.

At times, I would get myself so worked up that I would have to leave the house. I wasn't leaving for good, of course, but I definitely would disappear for hours at a time. Usually, I wouldn't tell her where I was going, which just added fuel to the fire. If I'm being completely honest, I'm not so sure that I did this merely to vent or express my frustration with her, though my actions certainly had that effect. On another level, I was taking off in order to punish her, to exact some form of revenge for how I was being treated. I tried to prove my points by robbing her of the one thing in our relationship that she seemed to crave the most: a sense of safety. By leaving the house, I was increasing her anxiety by forcing her to confront the depths of her loneliness and isolation.

The more I think about it, I was incredibly cruel.

CHAPTER THREE
On the Brink

Mainstream society talks a lot about finding Mr. or Ms. Right. Culture tells us that we've got to have somebody, anybody, any *body*, and if we don't, we had better get on it or risk being a 40-year-old virgin. Or worse—an old lady with no one for company but a den of cats. Surely, *that* must be the most horrible possible outcome, something to be avoided at all cost. Or so society tells us.

Consider this. If Mr. or Ms. Right were to walk up to you right now, wherever you're sitting reading this book, what would they look like? What would they be like? I once asked a group of guys this question, and got a host of answers that were exactly what I had expected. I got every cliché in the book.

"She'd have blond hair and blue eyes."

"Kind of my height, just a little shorter maybe. Kind of slim. Not voluptuous, but not… you know, the other thing."

"Curly brown hair that goes down to the middle of her back. Oh yeah, and C-cups."

"I'm looking for a beautiful smile, one that gives me that butterfly feeling."

Notice anything about these answers? First of all, we're trained to focus on the physical. Most of us are savvy enough not to admit we're that shallow, so when asked, we'll reply, "Beauty's on the inside, that's what counts." My point is that we're not looking for the right stuff.

So brace yourself for yet another cliché, and don't say I didn't warn you. You can't give what you don't have. Don't groan! We all want love, loyalty, intimacy, respect, compassion, and friendship, but we think we can get it by simply finding the right person. This ideal person is what we call "the complete package." We fool ourselves into believing that when we find Mr. or Ms. Right, he or she will embody all of these qualities we yearn for.

Not gonna happen. To find these traits, you need to be the love you want to receive. Again, it seems like the most obvious statement in the world, but you'd be surprised how easy it is to forget. By being loving, loyal, intimate, respectful, and compassionate, that's one way we attract others with those same qualities. An open heart is much more inviting and accessible than a protected one.

But I didn't know that at the time. To say that my marriage was unhealthy would be a massive understatement.

My feeling is that, from my wife's perspective, I was probably just a ticket out of her father's house, which she had been anxious to escape. While we were married, she felt deeply ashamed and responsible for much of the sadness in her family's household. Her relationship with her parents was as unhealthy as ours was together.

Her behavior and interactions with her parents should have spoken volumes to me about what our life together would be like. If only I had paid attention from the beginning, I might have noticed how she treated others, which is a critical question to ask yourself.

I vividly recall my wife being condescending and sarcastic with her parents over the phone early in our marriage. These conversations were completely derogatory and disrespectful. It never crossed my mind that the same verbal venom would be unleashed on *me* someday, yet it was only a matter of time before I became her new favorite victim. As far as victims go, I was completely unsuspecting. I didn't stand a chance.

Many young women end up with asinine men because they're captivated by the kind words and actions they use exclusively on them, and often on nobody else. That may not be something to admire, ladies. While their kind treatment of you may be "special," it might not be long-term. How you're treated by your mate at the beginning of your relationship is almost never an accurate barometer of how you'll be treated later. The passage of time will allow your partner to grow more familiar to you, and the more familiar they are, the more real they become. This onslaught of reality can be like a brisk gust of Arctic air ... sudden, unexpected, and difficult to shake off.

Save yourself some heartache and take an honest look at your partner's treatment of others prior to making a life-long commitment. It's not a guarantee, mind you; it's just something to watch out for. Don't be taken by surprise, like I was.

Coming from a tight-knit family, the level of dysfunction in my wife's immediate family was completely alien to me and I didn't know what to do to ease the situation. But there again was my need to step in and fix things, to be the hero in her life story.

A hero, I would never be. I could do nothing right. My wife didn't care for my friends and she grew increasingly critical of my family. With each infraction, a new and conclusive notch was stabbed into my belt of inadequacy. Add this to the World Series of scorekeeping, and pretty soon I found myself in the midst of the perfect storm. No marital mistake or blunder went unnoticed. She didn't let me off the hook for anything. She could be as immovable as granite and keep memories of Methuselaic proportions. Embattled and besieged, I felt truly hopeless.

Relationships are difficult enough as they are. When someone chooses to keep score, they're choosing to hold you to the mistakes of your past, an impossible standard. They never let you forget. None of us are capable of overcoming that kind of overt damnation. None of us.

So why do scorekeepers keep score? I can't speak to every situation or individual, but some people are simply that critical of themselves. Oftentimes, they have extraordinarily low self-esteem. They may not have connected to the beauty that is within them. Yeah, I know that sounds pretty corny, like something you might find on a Hallmark card, but I stand by it. If you recognize yourself in this description, you're reading the perfect book. Keep reading. Help is well on the way.

I was at least as needy and self-absorbed as my wife was, and in some areas I was more so. I married a woman that helped me to punish myself and treat me the way I felt I deserved to be treated. I had no sense of value and self-worth apart from my relationship with her, so it should have come as no surprise that her behavior toward me soon matched my own opinion of myself. In our neediness, even when we were at our most self-destructive, we attracted each other. Sadly, we were not the only couple to be trapped by this kind of experience. I believe it to be a common scenario.

After a year, I approached my wife about getting marriage counseling. She refused outright, unwilling to even consider the possibility. Having majored in psychology in college, she claimed to already know anything a counselor would tell us. Therefore, no amount of counseling would help us or change our situation. Walking away from multiple requests, I felt so helpless. In the absence of professional help, I knew nothing would change. At least, not for the better.

CHAPTER FOUR
Freefall

Around the time of our first anniversary, my wife informed me that an old friend of hers was coming into town. She admitted to me that she had once been attracted to him and wanted permission to be able to go out on a date. Huh? I was so confused. "Sure," I said without taking enough time to consider the ramifications of what I was opening the door to. But I had one caveat: "In return, you have to let me go out with another woman, too."

Relationally, we were already teetering on the brink, but I think this was the specific point where we leaped over the edge and went into freefall.

There was a girl from my volleyball league I had been flirting with. In my mind, our banter was entirely harmless. We shared some fun times together, but had started forming a few too many emotional bonds than was appropriate. But like so many of the mistakes I was making, I lacked the courage to identify my errors for what they were: selfish.

With my wife's proposition, I realized I had been presented with a golden opportunity. My mind immediately went to the girl I'd been flirting with lately. As soon as my wife agreed to the deal, I called her to set up a date.

Because of the way the timing worked out, I ended up going out on my date first. The girl and I had dinner and drinks, then went out to a nearby park where I had planned a picnic. It was all very romantic, though these were things I would have preferred to do with my wife. In any case, I enjoyed planning the day and making it special, and since I knew I would be returning to my marriage immediately afterward, I made the decision to make the most of this opportunity. So it was that, after polishing off a bottle of wine, we had sex.

Just like that, I crossed a line I never thought I would cross. I could hardly recognize myself from the man I had been before meeting my wife. I had all the excuses in the world to justify what I did. In my head, I had no trouble talking myself into it. I was hurting so badly. Emotionally, I was bleeding out on the table and my wife wasn't doing anything to stop it. I thought that if I slept with another woman, my wife would get the hint that we needed help. I thought this might be our ticket into marriage counseling, and if it worked, then surely there was nothing wrong with the brief affair. I was hoping that she would be profoundly hurt by my actions, and if she was hurt badly enough, maybe she would recognize how much I was suffering in our marriage. I was worried that she would later sleep with her date as well, and I didn't want to get left out of the "fun." If she was already planning on getting some retaliation against me, I was determined to strike first.

Let me step out of this story for a second and concede, yes, this whole situation is *unbelievably ridiculous*! I'm not blind to the morbidly convoluted mindset I'm demonstrating here. It completely reveals what hurting people are capable of.

You see how easy is it to get lost in excuses and rationalizations? Out of our own pride, we often build emotional walls between ourselves, give silent treatments, and neglect to articulate what we really want. I wanted my wife to understand the hurt and pain I was going through, but inflicting her with more of the same simply wasn't the way to get her to connect to my plight. For that, there would have been far better ways, though perhaps less pleasurable ones in the short-term.

I couldn't take the guilt. I couldn't look myself in the mirror. I couldn't keep quiet.

A few nights after this indiscretion, my wife started to grow unusually amorous with me. The sickening grief overwhelmed me until I stopped her and admitted my wrongdoing. Of course, my initial poor decision was now made worse by horribly atrocious timing.

To add insult to injury, when her date came up on the calendar, no romance resulted. This further infuriated my already distressed wife.

I was plagued with remorse for what I had done. How could I not have seen how poorly conceived my plan was from the start? I knew our marriage wouldn't be able to take the infidelity, and I couldn't handle being responsible for the downfall of our entire relationship. But it was too late. Our freefall was occurring at alarming speeds.

Shortly thereafter, I was working on a paper for RockWater. When I was finished I asked my wife to proofread it for me, since this was something she was quite good at. Instead of printing it out, I left it for her to find on my computer.

I guess I could have been more careful.

While she was on the computer that day, something caught her eye in my email account. As she continued to investigate, she uncovered my involvements with an adult sex partner website. In fact, she found my involvement to be more than idle curiosity. I had been exchanging messages with other people on the site ... and not all of them were women.

When she was done, she confronted me in the living room. "Is there something you want to tell me?" she asked.

I didn't know what she was talking about, so I declined. My wife got my attention with a right hand slap to the face. My heart pounded, face flushed and palms sweaty. Immediately, I knew exactly what she was talking about... and I couldn't fault her for it.

As it is with all things, my indiscretion was actually quite long in the making, even before I was married. I had planted seeds of lust and desire long before real opportunities presented themselves. Mentally, I had played out multiple scenarios and fantasies over the years. The internet provided me with a means of exploring sexual possibilities that I wouldn't have otherwise had access to or been comfortable pursuing. Challenged with a troubled marriage and feelings of rejection, I went deeper into my addiction than ever before. My coping mechanism was porn.

Here's an interesting thing about pornography: there's never enough. I longed every minute of the day to get off, to have a moment of relief, only to discover that each and every time I was left a little emptier than when I started. Pornography drains you, leaves you dry. Of course, this was something I had to learn the hard way.

When I felt terrible about myself, I retreated to porn, and ended up feeling even worse. Then I'd go back to the porn, only to walk away feeling more horrible than ever. My response to this would be to find even more degrading pornography, let my predilections go a bit further, a bit darker, a bit deeper... until I couldn't see my way back out.

When my fantasies began, they were limited to the computer screen, but they didn't stay that way. Pretty soon, I was yearning for my own physical experiences: bookstores, strip clubs, and video booths were only the beginning. The adult websites offered something more. Yet, as anyone who's been involved with these hook-up sites knows all too well, very few participants end up carrying through. Online, everyone's a tease. Most people are just there for the fantasy, which can be infuriating for the committed perverts who will do just about anything to make sure these discreet encounters actually materialize. By this definition, I was a committed pervert.

On some level, I wanted to get caught. I wanted off the ride. I wanted help. I just didn't have the courage to ask for it. Maybe that's why I wasn't careful about hiding the evidence of my online wanderings. Letting my wife discover my secret, on a subconscious level, was the perfect solution to my problem.

In the end, I got what I wanted. In light of my newfound dependence on pornography, she finally agreed to see a counselor. But whatever victory was inherent in this concession was extremely short-lived. After just two counseling sessions, my wife decided not to go back. According to her, she had made peace with me. The fence was mended. Supposedly.

A month later, she secretly made her retaliatory move. Unlike the first time, when she'd asked for permission to go on the date, she took advantage of the fact that I was out of town to commit the deed. Unbeknownst to me, she slept with a former college classmate. Just as it had been with me, though, it didn't make her feel any better. She felt horrible, furthering the challenges we had in navigating our relationship to safe harbor.

The details of this particular affair were unknown to me right up until the time of our separation. Despite not finding out the specifics, however, I seemed to have known that something was very wrong. I was out of town, attending a conference in Colorado, ironically spilling my guts to other men for counsel and help. When I talked to her on the phone the day after the affair, something about her tone didn't sound right. She was distant and aloof, more than usual. Her anxious protectiveness seemed to imply that she had something to hide. I recognized her defensive posture as a play straight from my own playbook.

Later, during our separation, a similar conversation took place between us over the phone after she took a trip to Seattle. There was no question by the shame resonating in her voice that she had been with someone. All she said was that she was tired. She didn't give any other indication of what had happened, but I felt it.

As a result of her actions, her guilt drove her to plan a surprise, secluded weekend for the two of us. This was something she had never done before and it only fueled my suspicions. Within a couple of months, I hooked up with another young lady myself, hence the cycle of destruction went unchecked.

Because I was continuing to see the girl I had slept with, in the context of the volleyball league we were both a part of, conversation arose as to whether I should quit the league altogether. My wife told me it was my decision, that she didn't want to take away something I enjoyed. So I continued to play the season out, further prioritizing my own selfish desires over my marriage. In doing so, I left my wife feeling even more devalued by yet another poor choice. And more indiscretions were to follow it.

If we were still in freefall, the ground was now rushing up at us at breathtaking speed.

In the last few months that we were together, we decided to get out of the apartment we'd been renting and buy a home. Perhaps we hoped that our problems would be solved—or if not solved, alleviated—by a change in venue. It seems strange that we should have thought a commitment to a house would mean anything. After all, our commitment to each other wasn't worth much. The worst damage had already been done. Nonetheless, we proceeded with the purchase.

We had just barely started unpacking when, one morning, I commented to my wife that she looked particularly attractive. I made the observation because she was wearing clothes that would have been more appropriate for a night out on the town than a day of teaching in front of teenagers at a nearby high school. My exact words were, "You look beautiful this morning." I meant every word of it. Conversely, I'm sure my wife meant every word of her response: "Of course you would say that. You're my husband. You're supposed to think I'm beautiful, but I want someone else to think I'm beautiful."

Since I didn't know what to say, I let the comment go uncontested. What was the point?

Within four weeks, I was told by my wife that we were going to go out with one of her fellow athletic coaches from the school. The plans seemed innocent enough, and I didn't sense anything amiss about it.

When the evening came, we headed out. In the car, she shared with me the odd fact that the guy we were meeting would probably be wearing a blue shirt. According to her, it was because the color complemented his eyes. I should have known something was up, but I had my blinders on.

That night, we shared a number of beers with the friend and then made our way back to his house after the bars closed. It was late and I was tired. By the time I sat down on the couch, my exhaustion overtook me and I allowed my eyes to close for a few minutes. I drifted off to sleep.

When I woke up, the room was empty. I had gone to sleep while the other two were talking, but now it was quiet... maybe that's what roused me. As I opened my eyes and starting getting my bearings, I heard whispering coming from the hall. Not sure what was going on, I stood up and followed the sounds into the bedroom. My wife was inside with the man whose house we were visiting.

At the same moment I approached the doorway, I noticed a reflection off the window. What I saw next seemed to occur in slow motion. As I watched, my wife aggressively leaned over and planted her mouth on his while he was trying to pull away.

Splat! I exploded inside from the impact of hitting bottom. My kneecaps literally started to shake with anxiety and perplexity. I would have screamed, but my mouth wouldn't move. In fact, no part of me would move. Except my kneecaps. I stood there silently, unable to tear my eyes off the horrifying scene I was witnessing. Did she know I was watching? If so, was she getting off on it?

After some time passed and I gathered enough kinetic force to move my legs, one in front of the other, I intensely, purposefully made my way down the hall and through the living room.

In the same way that I couldn't move before, now I couldn't stop moving. I frantically paced back and forth trying to decide whether or not I should race into the room and start breaking things—or heads.

In a rush of motion, I gathered my things, flew out the door, slamming it behind me, and plowed my way down the steps and across the driveway. Flinging open my car door, I launched myself inside, reaching into my pocket, removing the keys, and turning the ignition all in the same movement. With a squeal of tires, I sped down the driveway and onto the street without looking to see if there was anyone else coming.

I was already several blocks down the street when my cell phone rang. Keeping one hand on the steering wheel, I dug the other into my coat pocket, palming the phone and reflexively checking the display. It was my wife. When I put the phone to my ear, I heard her asking, "What happened? Where are you going?"

"I saw you!" I replied sharply. "I saw you kissing him!" It was almost a shout.

She immediately started apologizing profusely, asking me to turn around and come back to pick her up. My mind was a blitz of emotion and frustration, all of our pain mounting to a boil inside me. I thought about leaving her behind, but it occurred to me that if I left, more than kissing would possibly go on in my absence.

I spun the car around, driving like the crazed man I was and launched the car back into the driveway. My wife came running out of the house and jumped into the passenger's seat. No sooner had the door closed than I had the car out on the street and back towards home.

It was a grueling, agonizing drive back. I unleashed a verbal assault, an infuriated, self-righteous attack on her character, her motives, and what I had just witnessed going on before my very eyes. On and on we drove, my fury rising in seeming unison with the needle on my speedometer. My wife was pleading with me to slow down. Instead, I only pressed harder on the accelerator, pushing until my foot was level with the floor.

I was hurt. I was ashamed. I was relieved. I was vindicated. I was confused. I was angry.

I was messed up.

The closer we got to the house, the crueler, louder, and more intense my voice became. Out of my mouth spilled a barrage of vulgarities and accusations until I was screaming at the top of my lungs. We were stopped at the final intersection before getting to the house.

"It was nothing!" she defended. That was all I could take.

From the car, I leaped out into the cold winter air. The car was still running, my wife still inside. I couldn't look at her. I couldn't even be in the car with her. I couldn't even look at the car! I walked away.

"Where are you going?" she yelled from inside the vehicle. I didn't know. I just kept walking.

Unfortunately, I hadn't calculated the weather into my half-formed plan. It was freezing out. My teeth were chattering and I pulled my coat around me. I knew I wouldn't be able to get far, so I doubled back and headed toward the house. I couldn't go inside, not in the state I was in, so instead I went into the garage. By this time, she had taken the car the rest of the way, and it was now sitting empty, still slightly warm. I crawled into the backseat, thinking to stay there for the night.

But the residual warmth didn't last long. Soon, I found myself shivering in the back of the car. Though the garage did a great job of keeping the wind and snow out, the freezing temperatures were quite another. I couldn't stay there. Looking at the door leading into the house, I was faced with an impossible choice: freeze in the backseat of the car or go inside and risk running into my wife. Talk about a rock and a hard place.

Coming to the only possible decision, I sneaked into the house and slipped onto the living room couch as quietly as possible. I didn't want her to hear me. I didn't want her to come down. Just being in the same house was more than I could stand. I wanted desperately to fall asleep, but my anger wouldn't subside long enough for sleep to find me.

At some point early in the morning, while it was still dark outside, my wife came into the room and asked me to come to bed. I was reluctant and ashamed, but after little rest and more emotion than I could handle, I was too exhausted for words. We made our way back up into the bedroom and crawled under the sheets together. Somehow, inexplicably after all that had transpired, like a bad scene from *Monster's Ball* we made love for the last time.

Except love didn't have much to do with it anymore.

A few days later, she told me that she needed some space... from me. Even though her father had specifically instructed me not to do so, I suggested she go home to her parents' place for the weekend. Little did I know that this would be our last day together as a married couple.

The bottom line is that we were angry and humiliated. Both of us exhibited behavior and took actions that we regretted right away and wished we had handled differently. In the moment, though, we couldn't see the forest for the trees. We had lost all perspective. No matter what anyone in the throes of separation and divorce might say, most people come down with what I would call a case of the crazies. Some never recover.

This usually entails forming a social support group comprised of other singles and divorcees, most of them just as bitter about their own relationship debacles. These new friends provide a receptive audience to whom one can preach to the choir. I fell into this pattern, using people to escape my own problems, to feel like I wasn't at fault for my separation when I knew that I was. I spent countless hours at pubs taking on the self-destructive habits of the friends I now surrounded myself with.

So, what are the crazies, more specifically? I suppose the symptoms vary from case to case, but from my own experience I can attest to paranoia, stalking, public pronouncements of divorce, vast fiscal expenditures, near constant sleep depravation, clinical depression, dietary extremes, and self-destructive, compulsive activities that only served to mire me in further confusion and self-loathing.

I became especially fond of stalking. During our separation, I got into my car and drove around town late at night, trying to find out where she was, who was she was with, and what she was doing. The only possible outcome of this was self-inflicted pain and punishment. My self-worth was non-existent.

In the beginning, I tried convincing myself that I wasn't the problem. She was. If it hadn't been for her, my marriage would have been on track. She had dragged me down with her, taken me down a road I never would have traveled left to my own devices. I made myself believe that everything bad that had happened was her fault, and not mine. The more I talked myself into this ridiculous lie, the clearer it became that I had become an arrogant, self-absorbed man—and not just in the realm of my marriage. If I were completely honest, I had been on my way to becoming that man long before I ever met my wife.

It was a profound revelation. Through taking responsibility for all the chaos I had created in our relationship, I found myself on the path to self-recovery. This was only the beginning of that pursuit, but it marked the point of commitment I made with myself and my Creator to change from the inside out.

At a Sunday morning church service a few days later, I felt an impression to open my Bible. It opened to Isaiah 58:11-12: *"The Lord will guide you continually, and satisfy your soul in drought, and strengthen your bones; you shall be like a watered garden, and like a spring of water, whose waters do not fail. Those from among you shall build the old waste places; you shall raise up many generations; and you shall be called the Repairer of the Breach, the Restorer of Streets to Dwell in"* (NKJV).

I owned my part of the pain. It would be another two years before I truly realized the power of that decision.

CHAPTER FIVE
Post-Splat!

The timing of our divorce was almost movie worthy. The final papers went through on December 23, 2003—two days before Christmas. My entire family was out of town for the holidays and I was left alone. Completely, utterly alone. I spent Christmas morning in my living room, sitting on the floor beneath my decorated fake tree. There were no presents under it; just me, bawling my eyes out. That was the lowest point of my life.

Obviously, the silver lining of this was that I had nowhere to go but up, and though I couldn't find a single reason to celebrate that Christmas, I look back on it as a major turning point in my life. My transformation from there followed the age-old philosophy of "taking two steps forward, one step back." However you look at it, it was forward progress.

Officially divorced, my now ex-wife kept encouraging me to get out and date. Her exact words were, "It would be so cute to see you with someone." Though I'm sure the comment was well-intentioned and meant constructively, each word felt like a stab to the chest. Every time I ran into her, she twisted the blade deeper. Quite frankly, in the months following the divorce, I was still hoping for the sun and moon to collide, producing a miracle of Biblical proportions: our marriage restored! It would be the greatest supernatural act since the parting of the Red Sea.

But it wasn't to be, and even if it had happened, my motivations for wanting it were hardly pure. I didn't want my marriage to survive out of any sense of love for my wife—I still didn't know what true love really was. All I could think about was saving face. My primary rationale was nothing more than idle pride. After all, divorcees are second-class citizens, right? I felt like I had just dropped several rungs down the social ladder. Divorcee. The very word elicited a shudder, implying failure and shame. Nobody would ever want me again. I had too much baggage. I might as well have tattooed my forehead with a big letter "D" to scare off the masses. As far as I was concerned, I was no longer worthy or deserving of a relationship. Instead of my hoped-for miracle, the only thing parting would be the crowd of available women all around me, avoiding me like a plague victim.

In my mind, it felt difficult going out, subjecting myself to the public eye. As a result of my involvement with RockWater and the non-profit sector in general, I had a certain level of notoriety in my town. With each familiar face I passed on the street, I didn't know who knew what, who thought of me in a poor light now that I had a failed marriage under my belt. For the next two months, I was a veritable recluse. Just as my ex-wife had, my friends and family got on my case constantly about getting out and about, but it took a long time for me to feel comfortable around people again.

Finally, I forced myself out the front doors of my house and back into the social world I had previously come to dominate— this had once been my element, and I hoped for it to be again one day. I was asked to volunteer as a celebrity waiter for an event fundraiser being held by another local non-profit. Despite my initial hesitation, it was refreshing to be back in the scene I had loved all my life. To make things even better, not one person I encountered so much as asked me about my marriage. This filled me with the sense of freedom and confidence I desperately needed to summon the necessary courage to function again in public. Interesting how other people don't think nearly as much about you as you think they do.

As a celebrity waiter, I interacted directly with the dinner guests in my section. One table was particularly entertaining. It was a group of dolled-up women, all of them married—except one. With much encouragement from the single girl's entourage, we connected and quickly became an "item." I could hardly believe my good fortune. On my first venture out after the divorce, I had found a very attractive prospect.

We dated for over a year, and very nearly came to the point of marriage. Even though we drew the relationship out, I think I was somewhat aware the whole time that I was supposed to get out of it. Spiritually, I felt like I was developing in a different direction than the relationship was.

We broke it off several times during that year, only to find ways to put it back together again. When I decided to walk away for good, I found myself caught in the trap so many lonely people find themselves in. I didn't want to be alone. I couldn't face the idea of not being in a relationship. I was still looking for another human being to help me feel complete.

How many people sabotage their potential by making hasty selections in a boyfriend or girlfriend? A lot of people in my shoes sacrifice their dreams in exchange for the first opportunity that comes along to "have someone." It's a poor exchange.

By the time I was single again, I took a position as an assistant manager at Starbucks. But even though I was seeing some success in my new work environment, I was holding back part of myself, perhaps not wanting to be too successful. My heart just wasn't in it.

I believe those around me could easily sense the internal static within myself, the struggle to figure out what was coming next in my life. There was a small voice inside pushing me on to seek the real me, the true me. I felt a big change coming and wanted to leave myself open to wherever that change took me. Was it a new relationship? A new job? A new school? Would I be moving to a different city? As it turned out, all of the above.

But before any of that unfolded, another woman came into my life. She frequented my Starbucks location, always around 11:00. Since I worked just about everyday, I saw a lot of her. She completely captivated me. She was charming, brilliant, and funny, but it took some time for me to approach her.

One day I started talking to her while she waited for her coffee, and it turned out that she was really sweet. I worked up the courage to give her my number on a Friday, but I ended up waiting all weekend without hearing from her. I was extremely disappointed. Fortunately, she came back into the coffee shop the following week, as she always did. After another engaging conversation in which I found out just how driven and ambitious she was—more on that in a moment—she suggested giving me her number. "You call me," she said. "Don't wait for me to call you. You need to call." The more I found out about her, the more I understood why she needed me to make the next move: she was too busy to pick up the phone!

To begin with, she came from money. Her grandfather had been very successful with plastic moldings and had even patented a dozen or so pieces that were now used on Cadillacs. From that, he had made millions of dollars. That would have been intimidating enough, except that she was also studying to be a lawyer and was getting ready to take the LSAT (Law School Admission Test). Again, that was pretty impressive, but it was made more so by the fact that she had already been accepted to attend law school at Cambridge University, in England. Did I mention that she was taking flying lessons? She came over to Starbucks to study for the LSAT every day after flight school classes at the airport. She was also an avid runner, cyclist, and kayaker. I'm telling you, she was a bit manic.

We started to hang out, taking it slow. It wasn't anything too serious. At least, that's what I thought. Because of my state of mind internally, struggling with who I was, where I was, and how I wanted this relationship to define me, I became confused. It was one of the strangest and most debilitating experiences I have ever had as I watched myself in slow-motion go through total relational sabotage. This young woman had everything going for her... brains, talent, beauty, wealth, ambition. I kept asking myself: What does she see in me? Why would she want me? What a terrible series of questions to subject myself to!

Before I knew what hit me, I came down with another case of the crazies. I reverted to my old stalker mentality. I was suspicious of her other friendships, always wondering if she had other relationships going on. I was so paranoid. I couldn't be myself, no matter how hard I tried. For that matter, trying harder seemed to make things worse. I was a mess.

Despite my messiness, I was wholeheartedly seeking spiritual renewal. What in the world was my problem? It's hard to explain how these two conditions could have existed simultaneously. This is a time of my life I like to call "spiritual schizophrenia." For those of you who don't know what I'm talking about, it's a spectacularly confusing affliction. More on that in a moment.

I was coming unglued in my professional life as this was going on. At first, I wasn't able to perform reliably at work. Pretty soon, I couldn't even *be* myself at work! My schizophrenia was leaking out into all areas of life, and I couldn't stop it. It was like a train bearing down on me. My normally cool and collected exterior flew out the window. Patience? Gone. Humor? Gone. Confidence? Gone. I went from trusted employee to complete incompetent in no time flat.

Again, what the heck was my problem?

I was making a lot of stupid mistakes, but the straw that broke the camel's back finally came in May 2005. It was my responsibility to open the store that morning. As the assistant manager, I was the one with the keys. I was supposed to be at work at 5:15, but because I missed my alarm, I didn't even wake up until 6:20... I immediately called my shift manager to let her know I was on my way. I got ready faster than I've ever gotten ready in my life, jumped in my car, and sped off. The store was supposed to open at 6:00, so I was already unacceptably late. I was still a few minutes away when my shift manager called me back and told me just to turn around and head back home. "The district manager is coming in tomorrow. She wants to meet you at 10:00."

I was crestfallen, absolutely disappointed in myself. I knew what the district manager was going to tell me: "You're fired."

And she did.

Truthfully, it was one of the best things to ever happen to me.

●●◆●●

Who are you? That's the first question you need to answer for yourself. Not just any answer will do, though. In fact, everyone answers this question for themselves in different ways, but usually they arrive at a series of conclusions that lead to inadequacy and personal confusion. Trust me when I say that there's no room for inadequacy and personal confusion in a healthy relationship. I've tried it. More than once. Chances are, so have you. So let's try something different.

In *The Matrix*, Neo is challenged to see his true self. We end up asking ourselves the same questions. Though our reality probably isn't going to be that we've been living in an artificially-constructed holographic world in which our minds are trapped to keep us from discovering that our bodies are being used as human batteries to power massive cities occupied by machines that have taken over the planet, our own personal truth may not be any less surreal. Well, maybe a little less.

Why is it important to know yourself? Here it is, and you may want to highlight this: the way you see yourself determines the way you see other people. This being the case, how can you find your way into a quality, committed relationship if you don't perceive the mirror through which all the other people in your life, particularly your significant other, are reflected? If you're walking around confidently, feeling like a million bucks, then chances are you're going to see value in other people because of the value you see in yourself. Is this how you see the world? If it is, then sadly you're in the minority. Most of us are emotional and relational cripples, struggling to get back up off the mat after three or four divorce-proportion TKOs.

Whether you're brimming with value and worth or just barely keeping it together, you're going to treat every relationship accordingly. I can't be myself, share my opinion, or express my true feelings with someone if I think that what I have to offer is worthless. Instead, I'll most likely acquiesce, let the other person have their way in every conflict, and walk the lonely road to passive aggression and ultimate irrelevance. Or worse, I'll overcompensate and portray myself as powerful and aggressive, which will manifest itself as control, domination, and manipulation.

Until you choose to address your view of yourself, your relationships and experiences aren't going to change much. In fact, they aren't going to change at all. Problems in all forms of relationships, whether between friends, fellow employees, or marriage partners, will follow you wherever you go. You can run, but you can't hide. Unless you go to the source of the problem and make a correction, every relationship will manifest the same problems, only with different faces. You'll ask yourself, "Why am I always dating the same kinds of people?" The answer will be, "Because you're the same person with the same issues."

Whatever you have now, you're going to get more of it in the future. Experiencing a lot of pain, turmoil, confusion, and frustration? Get ready for a lot more of the same. Eventually, you'll come to a point where you come to expect failure long before it happens. Like all self-fulfilling prophecies, once this expectation sets in, it's almost impossible to reverse course. If I think I don't deserve or can't expect a quality relationship, I'll never find one. We don't see things as they really are; we see them as *we are*.

Unfortunately, most people can't accept this reality. After all, it's a heck of a lot easier to blame specific people and circumstances. At least those things are tangible. As long as there's everything wrong with the rest of the world, I don't have to deal with the complexities I look at in the mirror every morning.

To get off this painful cycle, I had to get incredibly brutal with myself: Same pain, different people. The only common denominator was *me*!

CHAPTER SIX
Spiritual Schizophrenia

There were days when I felt in control, and days when I did not. Days when reason and logic prevailed, and days when they simply evaporated. Days when I heard, felt, and embraced God, and days when I heard nothing, feeling isolated and alone.

I can't explain the discrepancies. All I can do is describe them.

There were nights when I'd go to the local pub, drink a few pints, belt out a few karaoke tunes, and then flirt with all female humanity. When I came home, however, it was another story. I'd be pacing the living room carpet until 3:00 or 4:00 in the morning, crying out to God, "What's my purpose? What's my reason for doing what I do? Where am I? Where are you?"

All I can say is that much goes into a person's life that they can neither explain nor nurture. It is simply part of the journey.

In my earliest season of grief, while I was mourning the loss of my marriage, I became a broken record. I would repeat the same contemplations, regrets, and complaints over and over again ... to anyone in earshot. My friends would offer to take me out for coffee or a meal, only to be subjected to the same old relentless dribble.

Yet, graciously, nearly all of them would patiently listen. They even offered a lot of sage advice, though I couldn't get to the point of implementing much of it. I felt incapacitated by my self-loathing. The pleasures of feeling sorry for myself seemed to excuse me from all the necessary responsibilities of normal human behavior. It was as if I believed that, because my marriage had tanked, I had a right to selfishly and abusively berate myself without care for the environments or conversations going on around me. In short, I was a Debby Downer.

Or perhaps, as a male, *Donny* Downer.

What's amazing to me is the caliber and loyalty of those who stuck by me. Even in my deepest depression, when I was self-hating and unbearably misery ridden, my closest friends— including my mother and father—showered me with grace and uncompromising love. They knew the real me even when I didn't, and they buckled down to love me through life's storm.

I had become that old family dog that everyone seems to have grown up with—the one you chase, pet, play, and love— that has gotten sick. That beloved creature becomes distant, bitter, and even snaps a bite at its own master. However, once the sickness begins to subside and the fever dissipates, the lovable, playful family dog returns.

Well, I was sick. Sick in mind, sick in heart, sick in soul. But my family and friends wanted to treat me, heal me, and most of all, save me from myself.

Just prior to my separation, I had gone to work for my dad. Perhaps this choice caused further complications to my marriage. My dad worked out of his house, so I spent a lot of time with him... and also my mum. We'd take walks around a pond near their home every day at lunch, talking and laughing the whole time. Perhaps working closely with my parents became threatening in some way. I honestly don't know. However, what became important was that I had these parents around me through the initial impact of separation.

My dad was a sales representative for heating and ventilation equipment, and I was an estimator—a very poor one at that. My emotions often got the best of me and I'd sit silently hunched over a set of blueprints, tears falling on the page, my chest heaving as I tried to hold back my irrepressible weeping.

From the other side of the office partition, my dad would pick up on my anxiety—whether it was heard or felt, I still don't know for sure. A couple of times, he even told me to go home and return only when I was ready. I would refuse, wanting to stay at work. At least the work kept me distracted. Well, at least that was the theory. The truth was that my work was suffering horribly, since I was nothing *but* distracted.

I couldn't eat. I couldn't sleep. I couldn't stop thinking about what a rotten mess I had gotten myself into. I became oppressed, even addicted to my own pain. These haunting, runaway emotions impacted every area of my life.

I had never been one for drama. I had never been one for depression. In fact, I have always been a person of joy, humor, and fun-lovingness. Yet all of that was vacuumed out of me. How could I have sunk so low? I didn't understand my own behavior. Who was this person I had become?

Despite my crap, there my parents were, faithful counselors, healers, and friends. I had these two wonderful people at my side revealing such amazing support and compassion during a time when I needed it the most. I heard about the challenges they had gone through in their marriage, issues that as a kid I never even knew were going on. My parents were honest with me, vulnerable at times, about what it takes to make a great marriage work.

If for nothing else, this entire experience opened up my eyes to the amazing world of parenting in ways I never dreamed. I was humbled, grateful, and freakishly in awe of their love.

So it was that my parents showed me great humanity at its finest hour. At the same time, I was also dialing into some other avenues of support I can only describe as supernatural. Here I was, learning so much about myself, my family, and even parenting. And at the same time, it was as if God Himself stepped off his throne in the big house of the sky and found a seat on my living room couch. Every now and again, he'd throw his arms around me and just squeeze.

One night, I wrote this in my journal, dated 9/24/03:

"Now that its been five months, where am I in the process? Lord, only you know. I am tempted to write my thoughts, but they are merely my emotions—and not at all the truth. I know that You are working in my life. I only need to trust You, sit tight, and be patient—all things which are so incredibly difficult for me. You know how much I want direction with this job, my living situation, and my future. Then there's the relationships in my life. Everyone that I depended on is gone. Only You are left to give me comfort, counsel, and contentment."

It's crazy to think that at the same time I was experiencing so much positive infusion, I was also partaking in ridiculous madness. But then, that's what makes this time of my life so unreal; the mystery of it all would be laughable if it wasn't so pathetic.

●●◆●●

One night, an old friend of mine was in town. He called me and told me that he was coming, that we'd go out, and with him would be a girl whom he'd been smitten for some time. The two were really good friends that never seemed to progress from that state, a state which my friend deeply wanted to transcend. I was to play wingman.

After several drinks, laughs, karaoke, and his introducing me to my soon-to-be favorite cigarette, Camel Turkish Gold, I headed to the restroom to relieve myself. The girl he brought followed me into the men's room, locked the door behind her, and proceeded to plant her lips on mine. I didn't really fight her off, so the kissing went on for a few minutes... mixed in with some groping.

My friend had seen us go in together, but surpressed his anger until a couple of hours later when we got back to my place. Once the girl had left the room, he called me out on this bathroom escapade. He asked, "Did you kiss her?"

"I did."

"Did you touch her?"

"I did."

His eyes welled up, his face grew flush, and his fist clenched. My poor friend was so hurt, so angry and humiliated. "Everything in me wants to come over there and beat the living crap out of you!"

I responded blankly, "I wouldn't blame you if you did."

Our friendship was instantly annihilated. This wingman wasn't such a good one, huh?

Why? Why? Why was I such an idiot? Why would I do that to my good friend?

My old friend and I haven't spoken since.

●●◆●●

That old cliché "one step forward, two steps back" seemed to really make a lovely home in me during this phase of my life. One moment, I thought I was truly embarking on tremendous growth. The next moment, I was a sunken ship of despondency, going nowhere but down.

I vividly remember certain individuals in my life saying, "In two years, you'll be in such a better place." Are you kidding me? I couldn't even imagine the coming week! I felt as though my organs were collapsing under the weight of my self-pity. A part of me just wanted to lay down and die in that boulevard of brokenness. Giving up would have been such sweet release…

I really just wanted to die.

Yet at other times, I'd be hard at work at my house, full of purpose: sweating, creating, building. One can draw much satisfaction from the labor of one's hands. I built a new deck, installed landscape blocks around my planters, laid some paving stone, posted a new fence, and even painted the inside of my kitchen cabinets. These days were extremely fulfilling.

I had other happy days, too, specifically when I was counseling other hurting hearts. I amassed many hours with friends and strangers who'd been hurt in their relationships. And there I was, in the midst of their pain, doing what I could to encourage, uplift, and exhort them from their predicaments.

Isn't it interesting that, though I could help others in their chaos, I struggled to grasp the answers in my own? Even still, I do believe I was learning. Learning the lingo, the language of love. Learning the psyche, the mindset of love. And even learning the heart, the emotion of love.

Some days, I was elated with my findings. Most days, unfortunately, I would have much rather stayed in bed.

But at least it wasn't *every* day.

One Sunday morning, I showed up at church to lead the worship band. I'd been out all night and hadn't even taken the time to shower. The sweet aromas of liquor permeated my pores and mixed with the stale, musk scents of bar smoke in my hair.

When the music faded, I walked off the platform where my mother was waiting. She lovingly wrapped her arms around me, looked straight into my bloodshot eyes, gave me a tight squeeze, and whispered in my ear, "Honey, why don't you just head home and go to bed?"

I was dismissed of my duties, but I wasn't dismissed as a person.

I wanted God. I wanted peace. I wanted sanity. I just couldn't get Him to work in my life. Somehow, I thought I had messed up somewhere, committed some unpardonable sin, resigned my position or place. I had no idea how I could ever be loved, how I could ever be trusted, how I could ever be valued... ever again.

Voices echoed in my mind, battling for dominance in my head. Which voice was I to trust? One moment, I felt together. The next, I was falling apart. I struggled to gain momentum as my emotions grew numb. That fight or flight impulse that we all have inherently built-in was drowned by my self-hate. If someone had wanted to punch me, like my wingman friend, I would have let them. At least then I could have felt something.

In my alone time, I would find myself prostrate on the floor of my living room, tears drenching the carpet, alone, quiet, and in awe. Like a two-year-old child, I would run rampant with energy, a flurry of emotion and protest, screaming at the ceiling, punching pillows, slamming down chairs, all in an expression of frustration. I cussed at God. I made accusations at Him. I blamed Him!

The problem was that I had seen too much of God. In my years of following Him, I had witnessed literally thousands of lives rocked by His compassion and grace. I knew there was a real and tangible God. There was no question in my mind.

Somehow, some way, God always showed up in the silence. In those times, I came to the end of myself. There He was... waiting on me. He was patient, loving, forgiving, and kind. He never made me feel inferior or weak. Instead, it was as if He was saying, "Are you ready to learn my ways yet? Or are you going to keep spinning this merry-go-round on your own efforts? If you want, I'll stay her while you take another trip around. If not, I can take over from here. Your call."

As much as I ranted and raved, I always ended up on that floor, exhausted, humbled, broken, and grateful for another day inching closer to the discovery of peace.

A few days later, I rationalized my way into treating myself to a last hurrah: Spring break in Cancun. What better place was there to lay everything on the table and truly purge my system of ridiculous thought processes?

Once again, the theory didn't quite match reality. I don't know why I thought this would be a good idea. I don't know why I didn't go with a friend or family member.

It was five days of poor choices, and fortunately, I didn't require any topical creams upon my return.

Yet again, I ask myself, "Why?"

When I got home, I was no better off than before I left. Sure, I had some new taudry stories to tell, but the hollowness of it all was becoming deafening. I was ready to explore the next step of my life minus the schizophrenia. I was sick and tired of being sick and tired. I was done.

CHAPTER SEVEN
The Things We Tell Ourselves

On my fifteenth birthday, my twin brother and I decided to play a childhood favorite with all the friends who had shown up for the party: Kick the Can. We were flying around the immediate neighborhood, scampering from bush to bush.

At some point, several of us had gotten caught and were found sitting on ghouls, the name we gave to our front porch, which was serving as home base. By the way, the *s* is silent, and for the record, I don't know why we ever called it ghouls. We just did.

Suddenly, my brother decided to be a hero and make a break for it.

According to the rules, if someone made it to the can and gave it a kick before the person who was "it" could call their name, followed by "One, two three," then everyone on ghouls— the steps—could run free. My brother was coming from the eastern neighbor's house, which was elevated about three or four feet higher than our yard. Between our homes, there was a small retaining wall and a medium-sized hedge. As my brother came flying through the air, attempting his finest Olympic hurdler impersonation, his shoelace got caught in the branches of the shrub.

With all the grace of a water buffalo, my bro came to a screeching, mid-air halt. His feet gave way beneath him and the rest of his torso rapidly succumbed to gravity's cruel design. He crashed to the ground, legs and arms tangled in a heap of indiscernible human flesh. His forearm took the brunt of the fall.

In a matter of minutes, the party mobilized and soon found itself relocated from the suburbs to the emergency room. It turned out he had a broken arm, and we waited for the cast to be set. It wasn't so bad, really. We pilfered out all of the powdered apple cider and hot chocolate packets we could find from the vending machines and, following directions, simply added water. We contentedly sat, gazing at the wall-mounted television, which was airing live coverage of a beauty pageant. I'm not sure which one it was, Miss USA or Miss America, but needless to say, this pack of fifteen-year-old boys sat transfixed.

We were definitely of age to appreciate a beautiful woman when we saw one. It's hard to believe now that most of them were only a few years older than us, but there they were, in full array, propped up, painted, and proudly displaying their glitzy sashes. Each one had a title, representing their states, and boy did they do it well—I mean, those Q&As are tough!

The irony of all this is that later in life I would place a sash upon myself, though a figurative one, a title of my own design. Unfortunately, my title wasn't as glamorous or dignified as "Miss California" or "Miss Wisconsin." No, I dubbed myself "Mr. Manwhore." In my own mind, with my misadventures in Cancun still fresh in memory, I easily beat out the competition.

Shakespeare wrote in *Romeo and Juliet*, Act II, Scene 2:

> Tis but thy name that is my enemy;
> Thou art thyself, though not a Montague.
> What's Montague? it is nor hand, nor foot,
> Nor arm, nor face, nor any other part
> Belonging to a man. O, be some other name!
> What's in a name? that which we call a rose
> By any other name would smell as sweet;
> So Romeo would, were he not Romeo call'd,
> Retain that dear perfection which he owes
> Without that title. Romeo, doff thy name,
> And for that name which is no part of thee
> Take all myself.

What's in a name?

Throughout life, I've given myself several titles and moni-kers. Sometimes I was a hero, sometimes I was a soldier, and still other times I was Wayne Gretzky. Almost all of my titles during my younger years were positive ones.

Many years later, those titles became less flattering. Judge. Liar. Cheat. And, of course, Manwhore. Whenever I wore one of those negative titles, I acted strangely, different than the person I knew that I was. Like a self-fulfilling prophecy, I mandated my behaviors through my own self-perception. A snowball effect ensued, and I soon found myself in a mass of confusion, fran-tically spinning out of control.

I remember regurgitating my own pathetic dating progres-sion to some friends a few years ago. One of them jested about my "manwhoreish" ways. Well, apparently that label stuck. It was at that moment that I placed upon myself my own sash, title, and definition. It wasn't true, it wasn't the real me, but it reflected the way I thought about myself.

Manwhore. In the days of old, this term was given to male prostitutes. I can't say that I ever received any cash for my services. I wouldn't have even been sure where to start the pricing!

In any event, in today's pop culture, the term manwhore means something much more common. Here's an anonymous posting from a girl on Yahoo Answers for the definition of this term:

> A manwhore is a master of manipulating women, and makes it his personal mission to sleep with as many different women as possible. As a manwhore, he also has virtually no emotional attachment to any of his victims. A manwhore's reputation, however, makes gaining potential new victims somewhat difficult. However, even in familiar environments, many manwhores can continue to get laid by playing the "I'm misunderstood" or "I'm just pissed and acting out over a bad breakup" card.

Well, by that definition, I lined up almost perfectly.

It was never my intention to walk down the road I found myself on. I hadn't exactly conjured this all up from a happy childhood dream: "Hey, what if I live really honorably throughout my twenties and then, when I reach the age of thirty, throw the world for a loop and slowly self-destruct to the bewilderment of all standing by?" Yeah, that's a terrific idea.

On a deeper level, I think people in general are not designed to handle guilt—certainly not guilt of this intensity. It's a debilitating emotion that corrupts us, short-circuits our potential, and destroys our identity. Yet rather than confront, we run.

I ran.

I remember beating myself up over and over again, rehearsing the same old lines ad nauseum: "What have I done? How could I have done that? What might I have done differently? Is there anything I can do to fix this?" All these questions inevitably gnawed away at my time, my energy, my psyche, my emotions, and yes... my sanity.

Ultimately, I had to face the truth: I can't change the past. I can't expect to ever be forgiven from those I've hurt, but I do have to forgive myself.

Like most of us, I was far more critical of myself than anyone else was. Perhaps worse, I allowed my shame and guilt to define me and fuel my propensity for self-destruction. I would say to myself, "Hey, I've gone this far, why shouldn't I just go all the way?" Blowing it in one area of my life had a trickle-down effect that eventually spilled into all the other areas, sabotaging relationships and opportunities everywhere I looked.

So when it came to relationships, my heart had grown defensive and protected. I was insulated from the whims of other people's opinions and the chafing of my own conscience. There was something cold about me, and I knew it.

Of course, I wasn't going to let anyone else see this. I would simply put on a mask and fake my way into the good graces of another pretty smile. After all, isn't that what we all do in the Westernized dating circuit? Two people *always* portraying themselves in the best light possible? Let's face it. It's part of our nature to allure. But it's not necessarily in our nature to pretend... and this is what people do. What I did. We *fake* it!

Here's a scenario for you. Two people meet at the health club, the bookstore, local pub... well, quite frankly, it doesn't really matter where they meet, does it? They wear the right clothes, apply makeup to cover up all their physical quirks, and style their hair just so. We all know, intellectually, not to judge a book by its cover. But we do it anyway. In fact, we've turned it into a science. Let's call it Hook-Up Science 101.

So the first person, Fakey #1, says to the other, Fakey #2, "Would you like to get a drink?"

At this moment, the games begin. The two people—facades, actually—calculate, analyze, and do everything they can to monopolize the interaction like multilevel marketing gurus. In this case, the product they're pitching is the mask they wear, and they'll morph and position themselves into whatever they have to in order to *be* exactly what the other person is looking for. Chilling, isn't it?

So these two facades hit it off and soon progress to fakey dates, participating in fakey conversations, and indulging in fakey concepts of lust and infatuation... maybe even fakey-fakey love.

Unfortunately, these illusions never stand the test of time. The real people behind the masks eventually emerge. In marketing terms, we would call this the bait-and-switch.

Let's be optimistic and say that the masks stay in place for as long as a year. After all, anyone can fake something for a year, right? After that, though, all bets are off. The real personalities are exposed and revealed. Suddenly, the fakey relationship is rife with all-too-real rifts and conflicts.

"You're not the person I started dating!" Fakey #1 hypocritically accuses.

Fakey #2 snaps back, "You're not who you said you were!"

Crushing disappointments arise. Degrees of depression and grieving are experienced. Declarations are made to "never go through that again." However, a few months later—or perhaps even weeks—these facades join new health clubs, visit new bookstores, and find a new local pub. They set themselves up for new fakey possibilities. All of this because they absolutely cannot face the prospect of, oh dear God no, *being alone*.

I'm convinced that dating has become nothing more than the combined skills of marketing, networking, and experimentation. If these are your fortes, you'll be wildly successful in today's dating scene. But don't go patting yourself on the back; this is not a compliment.

From another perspective, I think some people deceive themselves by using masks to create realities that may not actually be true. We seduce ourselves into believing that we *are* something because of what we *do*. Just because you sing, that doesn't make you a singer. Just watch those *American Idol* contestants who stand up in front of Simon and unwittingly make fools of themselves, casting themselves as fodder for morning radio banter and YouTube mockery.

What you do in life does not define who you are in life. The role you play is not what makes you an important person: politicians, police officers, CEOs, actors, athletes. It's easy to find security in what we "do." People often form their masks from the validation of their education, corner offices, and income levels. So many of us are actually much more vulnerable than we would ever admit.

Isn't it ironic how so many of us try to hide our failures, insecurities, and fears when these same failures are actually plainly obvious to everyone around us? I personally fought so hard to look the part—no way was I going to allow anyone to see my failures—except that *so many people saw through my facade anyway.*

It was as if my persona was an egg, as fragile and delicate as an egg can be. I went to great lengths to protect it—padding it, insulating it, taking great care of it. What's interesting, though, is that an egg, if left too long, will sour. Have you ever smelled the sulfuric pungency of a rotten egg?

What if you put an egg under heat? If it's not broken, it will grow hard inside, whether baked or boiled.

I think an egg is useless with its shell is left intact. As a matter of fact, an unbroken egg serves no other purpose than to make a pretty decoration over Easter weekend. Though you'll have to discard that smelly mess in a week or so.

However, if that egg is broken, its ability transforms. It can feed the hungry, fluff up a custard, provide structure and tenderness to a homemade cookie… You see, an egg only serves a useful purpose once it's broken.

Thus was the heart of this man. It wasn't until I experienced brokeness that I truly became whole.

It was a freeing experience the moment I stopped judging myself, stopped with the negative titles and masks. I threw out the old titles and began to label myself with newer, more productive ones: Faithful. Confident. Honest. Good. Happy. Powerful. Creative. Leader. Friend. Loved. Loveable. It was a decision I had to make everyday.

And sometimes, I still have to remind myself to do it.

CHAPTER EIGHT
Open Heart Surgery

In the summer of 2003, while I was in the beginning stages of my separation, I attended a conference in Huntsville, Alabama. It was hosted by an author who had written a number of books that profoundly affected me and helped me to see hope in the midst of a seemingly hopeless situation. He had a small bible college that I was immediately interested in, but at the time I was too preoccupied with the chaos back home to give any serious consideration to moving away from Wisconsin.

Two years later, my situation had changed. My marriage had ended and I had completely sabotaged whatever possible relationship I might have had with the girl I met at Starbucks. I didn't like what I had become, a serial dater who gave himself away to any girl who paid him the least bit of attention. I was so desperate to avoid the onset of loneliness, I went through a series of debasing, meaningless flings. Nothing left me satisfied, and yet even in the middle of this identity crisis, I was trying to get the help I needed.

I had been reading a number of books by this author, Jim Richards, even while going through all of my stuff. The titles included: *How to Stop the Pain*, *Breaking the Cycle*, a marriage book called *We Still Kiss*, and the one that compelled me to sit under the teaching of the guy, *Becoming the Person You Want to Be*.

As soon as I got fired from Starbucks, my mind returned to the school in Huntsville, I began making plans to pursue the thing that was compelling me on the inside. I knew I had to go, had to heal, had to grow, had to learn. So I put my house on the market and headed toward my destiny.

In two weeks, I had relocated to Alabama in order to explore a school that was based on teachings I knew had the power to restore me to the confident man I was before my marriage.

One of my good friends and mentors, Ron Marquardt, was counseling me and asked, "Angus, what's your greatest fear?" I responded, "The fear of failure." He laughed at me and told me I was full of crap. Then he went on and said, "Your fear is not at all about failure. My friend, you're afraid of success. You're afraid of the change you know is necessary to become the man you see in your heart. You don't think you have what it takes to tackle your stuff."

I had a lot of work to do, and if anything was going to change, it had to start with me. I had two things to work on: my outside and my inside. In the spirit of that, I came up with ten strategies I could implement that would affect my outside, my behaviors. These strategies wouldn't be enough on their own, but like a critical patient awaiting life-saving surgery, they stopped the bleeding, and that was a good place to start.

1. Becoming committed to personal growth, and thereby relinquishing myself to the process of change. This had to be the first step. By realizing that the only factor in my life I had absolute control over was my own behavior and thought-life, all my other strategies came into focus.

2. Taking responsibility for myself, my actions, and my circumstances. I was no longer operating from a victim mentality.

3. Being selective about what I allow to influence me. This meant that I stopped watching pointless TV. I put filters on my computer to guard me from falling into the old porn addiction. I read books, pounded through personal development CDs, and subscribed to daily email resources that built me up and secured my identity.

4. Changing the caliber of my friendships. I stopped all contact with those jaded individuals in my life that didn't contribute positively to the new direction I was moving in. I made sure that my new friends were people who were just as committed to healthy growth as I was. These friendships were mutually beneficial.

5. Embracing humility. Instead of trying to hide my problems behind a veneer of perfection, I sought counseling and accepted that I didn't have all the answers. In doing so, I became transparent and open about my struggles.

6. Journaling. By writing down my deepest thoughts and feelings during tough times, I was able to pro-

cess beliefs inside that I would never otherwise admit to myself.

7. Recognizing the pleasure/pain principle. I saw people as nothing more than sexual conquests. I thought sex would give me pleasure, yet it eventually resulted in pain. On the other hand, personal discipline and accountability seemed to me too restrictive and inconvenient. I made a conscious decision to deal with the lust in my life. I started to look women in the eyes when speaking to them, turn my head when an attractive body part was in my sights, and avoid innuendos and self-indulgent flirting.

8. Dealing with shame. We, as humans, love to suffer. We might not admit it, but it's the truth. For some crazy reason, I wanted to be punished for what I'd done wrong in my life. I thought I deserved it, and became an experienced self-punisher. Instead, I realized that nothing I had done in the past disqualified me from my hopes and dreams for the future.

9. Choosing to forgive. I had let resentment build and build inside until I was about ready to explode or shut down entirely. Unforgiveness is debilitating! The freedom inherent in letting go of grudges and hostility towards others is truly life transforming. I didn't realize how heavy the burden was until I took it off.

10. Understanding the importance of my heart. This became my *main* underlying motivation. I would ask myself, "How will this affect my heart?" I dis-

covered that my choices, good or bad, would,
without fail, affect my thoughts and how I see myself. I didn't want to further complicate my future.

I can't emphasize enough the importance of cultivating a heart that is soft, yielding, and receptive. The heart is the seat of our person. ("He put his whole heart into it" or "I love you from the bottom of my heart.") We don't realize it, but we spend more time there than we do in our heads. We commonly believe that our decisions and beliefs are made and determined logically by our thoughts, but this is only a half-truth. In reality, we're missing a step. Our thoughts *do* affect our decisions and beliefs, but they are filtered through our hearts first, and the condition of our hearts determines everything.

When I was a kid, I used to spend my summers as a pool rat at a local country club. All day long, me and my brothers would tan until we were golden brown—our hair, on the other hand, would go bleach blond—and our extremities would prune. We spent day after day at the pool, and loved every glorious minute of it.

One of my favorite things to do was to order a Kit-Kat from the snack bar. The chocolate was always cool and chilled, since it came straight from the fridge. I didn't care too much for that. It was much more fun to unwrap the bar and let it sit in the sun for a while. Placing the chocolate on top of the foil, shiny side up, the bar would melt. When I returned an hour or so later, there was a gooey feast awaiting my chlorine-soaked hands. It was so much fun to feel the chocolate oozing down my throat and smeared all over my mouth. I lived to suck my pruned fingers clean of this decadent delight. Afterward, I would rake my tongue over the surface of the foil wrap to pick up every last drop of chocolaty goodness.

Amazingly, French fries never had this same appeal. As much as I love a good French fry, when they're left out in the sun for an afternoon, they harden and become stale. Surely, there is nothing tempting or pleasing about a sun-beaten French fry.

I bring this up because I recently noticed that there is an interesting correlation between my childhood experience and the condition of my heart. During all this relational chaos, I was asking myself if God had simply made me this way.

In Cecil B. DeMille's *The Ten Commandments*, the Pharaoh wouldn't allow the Israelites to leave Egypt. The Biblical account says it's because "God hardened his heart." This story caused me a lot of confusion. Why would God harden Pharaoh's heart to the detriment of His chosen people? I'll admit that this didn't make any sense to me, until I thought about my melted chocolate bar. You see, the same sun that hardens French fries, melts chocolate. If you think about it, the sun doesn't change from one situation to the other, and in the same way neither does God. The more I came to understand the dynamic at work here, the more I saw that the only thing that changes is the condition of my heart. Did I want to be hard and unyielding in response to God's love, like a French fry under a hot sun? Or did I want to be like my chocolate bar, soft and flexible? By choosing the latter, I found myself making new decisions and forming new beliefs. I became teachable and open to new views and perspectives.

The first several weeks I was in Huntsville, I cried myself to sleep every night in my dorm room. I wasn't crying out of sadness, but from a thankful heart. I was discovering how to face personal responsibility in healthier ways. I realized the only thing stopping me from embracing true change on a heart level was making a choice.

Here's one heart issue I dealt with: victim mentality.

I had to accept the hard truth that all the pain I had experienced in my life was self-inflicted. I had allowed other people to negatively affect my value and self-worth. It was little wonder that I got as messed up as I did.

It's difficult to describe the power of these realizations since they all came at me in such a short span of time, fast and furious. I came to terms with the futility of playing the victim. It may seem like an obvious truth, but really, what's the point?

I'll share with you a short story to illustrate. I call it the bird poop proverb.

When I was in the fifth grade, I went out with my friend Ben on his paper route. He had just unleashed another of his typical smart-aleck remarks as we both left the porch of some house. The two of us were gregariously laughing our way toward the street when, from out of the tree above, this black speckled clump of white goo hurled out of the heavens onto Ben's head. Ben turned to me with an incredulous look of horror. I slipped into an uncontrollable fit of hilarity. Ben was furious! He stopped in his tracks, dropped his newspapers, and pumped his fist into the air, screaming at the bird as it flew away nonchalantly, soon disappearing into a copse of trees. I was still wiping the tears from my thoroughly entertained eyes.

That really happened. Now, let's hypothetically take the story a little further. Admittedly, I didn't come up with this part all by myself, so it's possible you've heard a slightly different version of it elsewhere. Let's say Ben cursed the bird some more, but nothing came of it, so he picked up his newspapers and continued on his way. When he arrived at the newspaper office, the poop now dripping down onto his sleeve, he complained about the incident to the dispatcher. Taken aback by his situation, she offered him a towel to clean himself off, but Ben refused, explaining that it wasn't his fault the bird had pooped all over him. If anyone was going to clean up this mess, it was going to be the bird that did it! He continued into the office, setting his newspaper pouch down on her desk and taking a seat. When the other paper delivery boys threw him questioning glances, he hesitated, then told them about his ordeal. They also offered to give him a moment to clean up, but he refused, again saying that the bird was responsible to clean up the mess. Meanwhile, thin threads of poop were now dropping off his head, pooling into putrid white clumps on the shoulder of his new designer polo shirt. He didn't concern himself. The bird would be liable to get it dry-cleaned. He continued to get strange looks from passersby as he left the office. By this time, he reeked of bird poop, and as he boarded the bus, his fellow passengers gave him a wide berth. He tried to explain the situation to as many people as would listen, but knowing what had happened didn't seem to compel anyone to want to take the seat next to him. That night, he looked at himself in the mirror with disgust. The poop had now soaked down to the roots of his hair, caking to the scalp. The smell was worse than ever, so he dug around through a drawer until he found a nose plug to help reduce his suffering. When it came time to shower and go to bed, he decided not to shower, for fear of washing his hair and thereby cleaning a mess that was not his to clean. He went to bed, smearing the mess onto his pillow and sheets. No problem, he mused. The bird would take care of that, too.

Now, I'll confess that it's a pretty silly story. But really think about it. How many people are walking through life with bird poop on them? Just as foolish as it is to blame the bird, we lay the fault for our unfortunate circumstances at the feet of the people we deem did it to us. Think of how much time and effort we waste waiting for other people to fix the problems we have in our lives when we could just deal with it, wash off the poop, and move on. The truth is that the bird does what the bird does, usually whether I'm standing beneath it or not. People who are hurting tend to hurt others. It's nothing personal. It's just what they do in wrestling with their own issues. There's no sense in being victims, wallowing around as though we're nothing more than other people's collateral damage.

I picked up the proverbial towel and wiped off the poop. Coupled with my ever-softening heart, I was becoming more and more attractive every day.

My next major revelation was that we never end up with what we truly want when we pursue our own selfish desires. Selfishness, in fact, was the source of most of my pain. By only going after what I thought would satisfy or make me happy, I left myself incredibly vulnerable.

In the context of human psychology, I learned that the three greatest needs of mankind are receiving unconditional love, knowing that we are not alone (not in a spooky E.T. sort of way!), and having a sense of value and worth, a purpose. It is absolutely essential for a human being to satisfy these needs. Most of us look to get these things from other people, usually from a significant other. Sadly, by attempting this, we are always left empty and disappointed. We apply pressure and obligation to others in order to have our needs met. For me, I discovered that if I were to be truly fulfilled in whatever I was created for, I should somehow find truth in the one that created me.

I've come to believe that anything we do to meet these needs outside of the Creator's ability to meet them leads to some kind of codependency: we use people and things to get our needs met. Sadly, it's ironic that some even use God. Leaders and followers alike use Him for power, identity, and authority all the time.

That said, society at large is totally geared towards this kind of destructive behavior. Advertising exposes our lack. Politicians spout our needs, only to offer to take care of them. Entertainment makes us feel inadequate by comparing us to ideals of beauty we feel we can never achieve, offering products we desperately "need," The examples are endless. We live in a very emotionally needy society. So many people are looking to take; very few look to give.

When we think about addiction and codependency, our minds turn to the "dirty" examples: drugs, alcohol, pornography, and sex. What we usually fail to acknowledge are the "clean" codependencies: relationships, jobs, power, money, title, education, and status. Of course, these aren't the only codependencies, just the most common ones. Some people love the concept of being "the hero" while others enjoy "being needed." We think these "clean" codependencies are mundane. Normal even. We don't think about the damage they inflict on us unsuspectingly.

The irony is that the more I seek to fulfill my needs through *any of these* codependencies, the greater the needs become. Out of one pain, then, I continue the cycle of seemingly inevitable pain, like a hamster on a wheel chasing the ever-elusive prize at the end of his journey. All the while, my heart grows harder and harder, calloused by my own denial, guilt, and failure.

Having made the choice to face my stuff, I no longer felt trapped by the old snares I typically found myself caught in. Finally, after years of suffering at my own hand, I actually understood what it was that I was doing. It was so hard to see through my chaos, always blaming, shaming, and gaming to selfishly protect what I thought was important, my sense of being right, my ego, and my pride.

Throughout my first year in Huntsville, I found a staggering sense of clarity and wholeness. Slowly, I was becoming peaceful, confident, and alive—and I liked it! I really liked the person I was turning out to be.

My Journal—10/28/05

Greatness is never stumbled upon, nor inherited. It is a developed sense of self and an awareness of true identity.

Greatness is only found in those unafraid to succeed… for success demands a commitment to change, growth, and development; a commitment to the death of self and mediocrity; a commitment to excellence in who I am and what I offer to others.

CHAPTER NINE
Fighting the Instinct

It is said that relationships that last are often the same ones that are rooted in friendship. "Start by being friends," they say. In my first marriage, that was definitely a piece of advice I did not follow. Since my wife and I had crashed and burned, it occurred to me that if I was really going to take another shot at romance, I might be well-served to consider everything I did the first time around, and then do the opposite... George Costanza, anyone?

Now that I was taking a journey of change in my own life, I didn't want to immediately find myself in a relationship that would stifle it. Change, as I had learned, is not as scary or bad as I had once thought. So once I made the choice to undergo change in my personal life, I wanted to make sure I reserved my dating life for people who were as actively involved in the process of growth as I was. I wanted to be with someone who was willing to read books, choose mentors, and explore all that life has to offer in the area of personal development.

Growth attracts growth. As I began to see myself transforming and my weaknesses, inconsistencies, and fears began to fade away, I became drawn to others for healthy reasons and less attracted to people on the basis of filling my needs and inadequacies. In other words, I was attracted to others based on what I possessed, as opposed to what I didn't.

Everyone has flaws and quirks in their personality. Additionally, each and every one of us is at a different place in our life's journey. Because of this potential disconnect, we need to ask ourselves some important and challenging questions before we start dating: Am I willing to love this person just as they are, even if they never change? Am I ready to invite someone to join me on my journey? Have I respected a potential partner enough to deal with my own junk before entering a relationship?

The first step in dealing with that junk is identifying each of your character deficits. I know, that sounds ominous. The tendency will be to get down on yourself when you start to do this, but don't let yourself get demoralized. Your list probably isn't any longer or more extensive than anyone else's, just different. Such issues as detachment, irresponsibility, hyper-responsibility, perfectionism, and conflict with authority should be things you can both talk about together. Find people with whom you can be an agent of growth, healing, and change. Celebrate your journey, even though you haven't arrived. Positive growth doesn't just happen on its own; it must be regularly stimulated.

While I was in Huntsville, I limited my close friendships to fellow students in the college, people who had made similar commitments to change as I had. The friend who turned out to be the closest, however, was not a student.

Samantha attended the same church as I did. When we met for the first time, she was recently separated from her husband of ten years and effectively raising her daughter alone. We saw each other in a lot of group situations before it ever occurred to us to talk one-on-one. I had seen her around since she worked alongside some of my friends in the children's department. She seemed consistently "up" in her personality, which was a breath of fresh air. She was friendly and smiled almost all the time.

One night, there was a small group meeting at the home of some friends of mine, Clint and Sara. Throughout the evening, Samantha interacted with everyone very positively. I shared some of my experiences running a non-profit during the meeting, which she followed up on at the end of the night.

"My dad runs a non-profit charter school in Florida for Haitian students," she said. It was the first interaction I remember. Even more than the words, though, I remember the way in which she was able to engage with others so effortlessly.

Another day, about five weeks later, we were lounging around our church's café when I noticed her from across the room looking up at one of the TVs hanging from the ceiling. When I followed her eyes, I saw that the channel was set to the Spike Channel. I was momentarily puzzled, because I didn't know very many women who watched Spike, let alone the program that was playing that day. Namely, the UFC (Ultimate Fighting Championship).

In case you're not familiar with this particular brand of entertainment, it's a combination of boxing, wrestling, and martial arts of all different types and varieties. It's often coupled with the term MMA, or mixed martial arts. If I had to put a word to it, it would have to be *violent*. These guys strategically beat the living crap out of each other, and there aren't very many rules.

For instance, eye-gouging and biting are strictly forbidden. Groin attacks are a no-no. Other than a few basic caveats, though, pretty much anything goes. It's an amazing display of strength, stamina, and heart. UFC is serious business. If you look at the ratings and demographics for the pay-per-view events that UFC has become famous for the world over, and break them down by gender, I'm sure you would find numbers something like this: 95% men, 5% women. For the most part, women just aren't genetically predisposed to this kind of extreme combat.

Put aside the strange fact that I saw her watching this at church, and perhaps you can imagine the surge of curiosity that rose up within me. A couple of my buddies were standing around, equally amazed, and we couldn't help but marvel as she began talking about what she was watching, rattling off the names of the featured fighters and their stats like she was reciting a recipe for cornbread.

Who are you? I was asking myself. *You're a girl. You're not supposed to like this stuff.* The truth was that I had never been that interested in professional fighting, and this was no exception. I was a novice, a UFC virgin. It wasn't that I disliked fighting, I just hadn't ever thought much of it one way or the other. As I stood by, though, my friends started talking about it some more. It didn't take long for her to admit that she watched the pay-per-view fights every month at her house. Since we were all curious about it, we decided to each contribute a few dollars and join her for the evening. My motivation was less to find out about UFC and more about investigating this very unusual woman.

There were about fifteen of us that showed up on her doorstep that Saturday night, but if she was unnerved by our numbers, she didn't show it. As a true UFC disciple, I think she was just happy to spread the word.

I had a great time. It was more than just the fights, though they were really good. I can still remember exactly what was on that night. It was UFC 56. Rich Franklin was fighting Nate Quarry, and Matt Hughes took on Joe Riggs. I absolutely thrive in social situations… at least, I had before completely unraveling after my divorce. After all these long months and years, I finally felt like I was back to form.

The week after that first UFC experience, I made it a priority to find out anything and everything I could about how it worked, including the fighters themselves, the rules, the people behind the scenes, and the culture. Being an athlete myself back in the day, I knew a thing or two about wrestling, so I could connect with the tremendous underlying skill the fighters had to master in these varying styles. To say I was impressed with the stamina these guys portrayed would be putting it lightly. I had a lot of respect for them. Ultimately, I was determined that by the next fight night, I would be able to talk the talk.

Fortunately, I didn't have to wait a whole month. There was a UFC reality show broadcasting at the time, *The Ultimate Fighter*. This proved the ideal environment for me to show off my newfound expertise.

Our group also started watching American Idol together. Being a karaoke enthusiast, I felt I had a unique expertise in this area as well. I guess you can say we started bonding over reality television. So, despite the bad rap that reality gets nowadays— it's blamed wholesale for the brain drain of American culture over the last decade—at the very least, it brought Samantha and I together. The long and short of it is that before long I found myself hanging out at Samantha's place three or four nights a week. I suppose it was inevitable that we would start to get to know each other really well.

Now, I had made it a personal goal to stay single for at least a year. To see the change in myself that I so desperately needed, I had to remain focused on the goal, to keep away from any distraction. After all, I'd been in a string of bad relationships since my marriage. I had become a serial dater, a gigolo, prolific at one-night stands... a manwhore. If my instinct was to get into another relationship, even with someone as cool as Samantha, I had to fight that instinct. If I was sure about anything, it was that my instincts were often wrong.

My instincts were always to pursue and, like a chameleon, be the person I thought my love interest wanted me to be, but, you see, whatever you do to get a partner is exactly what you're going to have to do to keep them. It was good advice then for starting my new relationship, and it's still good advice. You have to attract instead of pursue. This is why most relationships don't work out. In the dating process, we often don't date other people so much as the masks they wear. But that should come as no surprise to anyone who's spent any time "on the market."

So I took it slow, so slow in fact that I didn't feel like we were going anywhere at all. We were friends, nothing more. Period. The end. I was careful to avoid any sign that things were becoming more complicated. I even made sure that we didn't spend too much time alone together. It helped that the vast majority of the time we saw each other was in the midst of a lot of other friends. In group settings, it was easy for me to keep things casual.

Do you remember your parents ever telling you not to hang around with certain friends when you were in grade school? I heard it a lot... didn't listen too much, though, even years later.

I would often jump into bed with my eyes and ears closed to all the warning lights flashing around me. Those lights were so bright and insistent that it sometimes took an impressive display of ignorance to block them out. Now that I'm older and wiser, I understand what my parents were getting at, what they really wanted for me. What they knew, and I didn't, was that people imitate those with whom they associate.

I started observing who this girl spent time with. It helped that we had some mutual friends that I respected. They always spoke very highly of Samantha, and even showed signs of being protective of her. I definitely took notice of this Samantha Fan Club. These people revealed what kind of woman she was, and so far the verdict was a good one.

A person gives time to those pursuits which they find important. If they spend a lot of time with family, they value family. If they spend a lot of time at work, they value work! Are they involved in volunteering their time somewhere or are they often at the spa? Do they exercise regularly or lounge in front of the television? These details are not meaningless and incidental; they tell a crucial part of their life story. Time is the most valuable commodity a person possesses. Don't believe me? You can always get more money, but time is something you can never get back.

So how did Samantha spend her time? She invested herself in helping others. She served in the children's ministry, organized a group to help at the homeless shelter, and participated in the young adult group at church—not to mention that her nine-year-old daughter was in tow most of the time. I sometimes wondered if she was too good to be true. But she wasn't.

It was becoming more and more difficult to restrain my burgeoning feelings for Samantha. Our friendship was rock solid, something I'd never shared with a woman I was interested in before. I was exploring new relational territory. This is how I came to realize that the cliché was true: the healthiest relationships begin as friendships. Although it might seem obvious in retrospect, I had never thought to try it. Impatience and loneliness always got in the way.

Life got difficult a few months into most of my relationships, when the romantic blinders started to come off, when I found I had to actually work to keep things together. When people don't have friendships to fall back on, they usually just fall apart and go their separate ways. Without friendship, they blame each other and take out their frustrations on one another, often in extremely hurtful ways. This is because they may not love and respect each other the way they think they do. On the flip side, you would never do anything to hurt or damage your best friend. You wouldn't crap on their parade. You just wouldn't do that. Friendship isn't just important, it's fundamental. It's the key.

By now, Samantha and I were best friends. And then, out of the blue, I made an unexpected realization about her: she was incredibly cute. Pretty soon, she was more than cute. I couldn't look at her the same way anymore. At first, I was taken aback to have had such a strange thought about my best friend.

One night, after all of our other friends left, Samantha and I were alone sitting on the stairs leading down to the door of her apartment. We were talking as I was preparing to take off when the words slipped from my mouth that I thought she was really attractive. To my surprise, she reciprocated. I was floored.

Without really looking for love, I found it, amid meaningless reality television and mind-boggling violence, of all things.

The only question still lingering on my mind was this: where do we go from here?

CHAPTER TEN
Control Freak

I was only supposed to be in Huntsville for one year. But you know what they say about best laid plans... the more I got to know Samantha, the more certain I became that I had to stay longer to explore our relationship. So my internal struggles continued. Was I doing this for the right reasons? How long would it take for the other shoe to drop? Was I going to revert to my old ways and sabotage this relationship, too? Was I willing to allow this relationship to develop in its own time, or was I going to try manhandling—manipulating—it like all the others?

These thoughts, I've come to believe, were vital to my own development. A baby won't crawl if you never give them an opportunity to give it a try. I had to push through my old ways of thinking. My mind would say one thing, but my heart another—which one would I listen to?

Early in my separation, I had bought tickets to go to a Dave Matthews Band concert. My real motivation for doing it was to see if my wife would join me. After all, it was her *favorite* band. I was sure she'd say yes. From there, maybe I could rekindle some of the romance. What was I thinking? Say it with me, boys and girls: MA-NIP-U-LA-TION.

When I invited her, she turned me down. I was devastated. As you already know, all my efforts at manipulating my wife back into my arms failed miserably.

But I wasn't going to waste perfectly good concert tickets, so I got a couple of my buddies together and went to the show anyway. The show itself was a wreck for me. I kept excusing myself to "go to the bathroom." Which was code for, "Please excuse me while I find a dark corner to sling some snot and have a good cry." It was dreadfully punishing to hear all those songs, one after another, reminding me of times past.

When the show was over and the whiffs of funny-smelling cigarettes waned, we camped out at my truck to await the lengthy exodus of vehicles from the parking lot. We had anticipated this, having packed lawn chairs and refreshments in preparation for what was known to be a two-hour ordeal at this particular venue.

While we were hanging out, we struck up a conversation with a group of young guys next to us. Interestingly enough, I started talking to one of them about our mutual desire to experience change and personal growth—I know, not the most likely place to find a therapy buddy, but sometimes life's like that. The guy confided some of his own stuff, and revealed that we had some things in common. Before we left, he shared about a book that he had been given, *Wild at Heart* by John Eldridge.

I laughed and then recounted my own experience of reading through the very same book. My counselor had recommended it to me several months earlier, and I had read through it, taking extensive notes that filled up entire notebooks. I told this young man that the book had helped me to realize just how dumb I had been. It had revealed all my ugly, selfish tendencies and behaviors, inspiring me to face my stuff.

Right there in the parking lot, the young man teared up, because it turned out that he couldn't bring himself to read it yet. He would start, get confronted, and then cowardly put the book down again. I acknowledged the difficulty of dealing with our own "stuff" and encouraged him to go for it. In the midst of a group of perfect strangers, this kid was hugging me and snotting all over himself as he finally found some encouragement to face his inner demons.

Days later, I remember sitting across the table from my wife, sharing the same story. As I retold this account, her eyes filled up with tears, obviously deeply affected. I don't think it's easy for any of us to deal with our really deep heart issues.

In all honesty, though, my motives in sharing that story were hardly pure. Here I was, arrogantly trying to persuade her to change—again. Throughout so much of my separation and divorce, I was still doing the same old things, attempting the same old tricks. I was still doing it to manipulate her! What I came to learn about myself was that I was a controller.

Controlling people comes in all different shapes and sizes. Whether it's passive aggressiveness or bold intimidation, it's all about manipulation. In some form or fashion, I wanted to have a hand in establishing my own desired outcome in the marriage. Even the Friday before our actual divorce proceeding, I sent her an email with all of my reasons for *not* wanting to get a divorce, as if guilting, shaming, and controlling were going to magically solve the problem. Even if it had worked, it would have only been a temporary fix and we would only have found ourselves back in the same place eventually.

Why did I even try this? I had no idea why, I just did it. Call it instinct, desperation, self-preservation... Ultimately, the *why* of it isn't important. Asking *why* is almost always the wrong question. Why am I like this? Why do I do the things I do? Why can't I move on and get better?

Was it because I had a babysitter abuse me when I was three? Was it because I was caught "playing doctor" with the neighborhood girls when I was still a kid? Was it because I found a stack of discarded *Playboys* when I was seven, and decided to look through them to see what all the fuss was about? Was it because I had lost my virginity, confessed to my parents, and then had no one talk to me for two days? Was it because that same virginity-losing incident had occurred at a church camp, and that the girl in question had moved on to another boy the very next night?

Getting the answer to a *why* question usually doesn't bring about healing and personal growth; it usually results in giving us something to blame, which then frees us to shrug off any sense of responsibility.

So forget the why. None of these things matter! Sure, the past can play a role, but none of those things were to blame. I had to take responsibility for the man I was. After all, nobody was making my decisions for me. The fact was, I liked the feeling of having power and control over another human being. Ten ill-advised minutes—okay, maybe five—at church camp nearly two decades earlier couldn't take the heat for that. The adult me had to fess up.

Still, the urge to investigate my own past proved irresistible, and as I started to trace my way back through my life, I discovered something about myself that had remained consistent over the years: I was a *huge* flirt. It started long before church camp and it was still going on. Mind you, I wasn't sleeping around my whole life… at least, not until I turned thirty. But the flirting had never gone away, not even when I was married.

Flirting got me the attention I desperately craved. It got me praise. It got me phone numbers! I had never thought anything sinister of my flirtatious nature, but the truth is that it was a predatory trait. Claiming female prey proved to be my ultimate personal, emotional validation.

When most people think of flirting, they picture a girl leaning over with a low-cut shirt or a guy pulling a Ron Burgandy (*Anchorman*), conveniently removing his shirt and flexing his muscles as a girl walks by. But I don't see these as acts of flirtation. I think they're acts of blatant desperation.

In my opinion, flirting is a series of subtle nuances that are highly manipulative. It can be a series of small touches, batting eyes, slight inuendos, kind favors, and playful bantering that can all contribute to an underlying danger: I use your emotions to satisfy my own personal deficiencies. And if you're really susceptible, you'll let me take advantage of you. That's where I amassed the greatest "sense" of self-esteem.

I was cold and calculating and didn't even realize it. It's shocking to me that I couldn't see this in myself at the time. At least I can admit it now.

But *why* did I want to control people and situations? Again, back to the *why* questions. In any event, the answer would be difficult, if not impossible, to adequately determine—and not worth the time needed to puzzle it out. However, I do know this: left to its own devices, my heart was dark.

Honestly, most of us are developmentally delayed in the major areas of our lives. We've never learned the proper skills to go about life effectively. What would be so bad about us all just admitting to our individual handicaps? I think we'd all be better off in the long run.

I finally got to the point where I recognized that it was not important to find out the answers to the *why* questions. Instead, it became my goal to understand *how* not to allow my handicaps, or issues, to dominate my life.

In Huntsville, my life was beginning to reflect these internal realities. Here I was, in a city that I had never imagined living in, attending a school that rocked my heart and perceptions in profoundly uncomfortable ways, attracting and meeting a girl who I often thought was out of my league... Well, let's just say there were a lot of potential variables to control.

As my journey unfolded, I found myself stepping outside of myself and becoming a spectator of my own behavior. When opportunities presented themselves to challenge my ego, my very person, instead of freaking out and taking control, I learned to simply let go. Nothing is quite as wonderful and terrifying as just letting go. By letting things be "out of my hands," I found the peace that had long eluded me.

Instead, I trusted. I yielded. I let go.

Since I had decided to stick around in Huntsville, I had a lot of things to trust God for. I needed a job, for one. I needed a new place to live. I needed to change my car insurance... indeed, God is in the little things, too.

Before long, I found myself at an insurance office, chitchatting with the receptionist. Between discussions about my insurance needs, I shared a bit about my non-profit experience with the receptionist. After telling her about RockWater, the young lady became unexpectedly excited and asked me, "Do you know Bruce Martin?"

I answered that I did not, to which she replied, "You should really meet him. He's starting something similar to what you're talking about." She scribbled down his name and number before quickly returning back to my insurance questions.

A week later, I still hadn't tried calling this Bruce Martin guy, despite the way he had been so emphatically described. No matter, apparently, because he soon called me. That receptionist had circumnavigated my long and admittedly unreliable decision-making process, smuggling my contact info out of the insurance agency and right into Bruce's hands.

We arranged a meeting over the phone, and it wasn't long before we sat together at a local Starbucks, me sharing all about my brokenness, failure, and divorce and him just listening intently. To my relief, his response was both inviting and inspiring. A smile crept over his face as he asked, "What in the world are you doing in Huntsville, Alabama?"

Four days later, Bruce's organization had its first meeting. I volunteered that first night and continued doing so for the next eight months, at which point Bruce offered me a job. Over a year later, I was hired as his replacement, serving as executive director.

After such a long struggle, indeed a seemingly endless one, I had finally been granted a second chance. I was once again where I wanted to be, running an organization I loved aimed at helping young adults. Except this time I had somehow avoided doing all the organizational tasks I hated, and wasn't any good at anyway: assembling a board, writing the non-profit IRS documentation, raising starting capital, etc. It was as if God had reached down and said, "Here you go. You wanted to know how easy life can be? Let me show you."

Here was proof positive that letting go was so much more fruitful than meddling and controlling. In truth, the only thing I can control is me. My thoughts. My motives. My actions. I was slowly relinquishing everything to someone far more capable and better equipped than I.

Those who think they can do it on their own end up obsessed with measuring their own moral muscle but never get around to exercising it in real life. Those who trust God's action in them find that God's Spirit is in them— living and breathing God!
–ROMANS 8:5 (MSG)

CHAPTER ELEVEN
Reconnaissance

I f you were to wander through my house, you'd find all of my tools in my garage hung neatly on a peg board. My sock drawer has white sport socks on the left, colored dress socks on the right. The black and silver kitchen utensils all go in one drawer while the wooden spoons, spatulas, and plastics all go in another.

Isn't it amazing how we'll strategize a stock portfolio, optimize a sock drawer, and calculate our March Madness picks, but hold very little regard for our relationships? We are so clever about *everything* else in our lives. Why are we so ridiculously flippant about who, what, and how our hearts are affected?

I think I treated the whole ordeal with a Wile E. Coyote concept on love. You know, pursuing your prey with an ill-planned, sure to fail effort that always leaves you crushed, exploded, or in many other ways hurt.

My heart was changing, and as the ol' saying goes, "If you want something you've never had before, you've got to do things you've never done before."

Sammy and I started seeing even more of each other. The difference was that now we were both being very intentional. We were on reconnaissance missions, exploring and taking careful, conscious observation of every detail. Both of us had been through a divorce at this point, and we weren't about to go down that road again.

It's important to know yourself before attempting to commit to a relationship with another human being. By knowing yourself, you're going to be able to attract other people who know themselves. This is critical to relational success.

But there's another aspect of knowing you'll need to be cognizant of: knowing who your potential mate is. Not just knowing their name and their job and what they like to do for fun. I'm talking about really knowing another person. Obviously, time is an important factor. The more time you spend with them, the more you'll find out about them.

Unfortunately, when getting to know others, most people resort to making judgments. In fairness, judgments can be made with the best of intentions. It's usually not malicious, but it's far too easy to observe peoples' behavior and jump to conclusions. Though you can observe behavior and tendencies, you can't pretend to know why they exist. If I see a man walk into a bookstore every day for a month, I might assume that he works there. Or maybe he's just an avid reader. Or maybe he frequents the coffee shop inside. The point is that it's impossible to know without asking him or gathering more information.

During our early relationship, about April of 2006, Sammy and I spent countless evenings in conversation and conflict. Some of you may cringe at the word conflict, but let me assure you that this was definitely the good kind of conflict. In fact, all that friction we felt early on served us well by generating a foundation of truth and honesty. We learned to never leave anything on the table, in the dark, or under the rug without dealing with it. No hurt or offense would be allowed to find harbor in our hearts. Although it was easier said than done, we marathoned our way through three, four, and five-hour conversations that, at times, left us exhausted and challenged.

It was during these personal interrogations that honesty found its root, and vulnerability its home. We found indescribable safety in addressing our own failings as previous spouses, while at the same time exploring the potential for what we could be in the future. All we had to do was check our "stuff" at the door.

Again, easier said than done.

Because of our previous marriages, we had to be bold and blunt with each other. Neither of us were anxious to set ourselves up for further hurt. We were both coming back from our lowest points, so in a sense we didn't have much to lose. We had everything to gain, though, if we could just get past our fears and continue our mutual investigation of each other.

Truth, in itself, can be at times destructive. Yet, when delivered through a filter of love, it becomes empowering, even inspiring. When two people are learning to open up to one another, great care is often taken to protect the areas of their lives they deem "delicate." At times, those things we attempt to hide end up coming back to harm our relationships later.

Life is full of difficult, delicate issues that we must share: having children, being diagnosed with venereal diseases, filing for divorce, dealing with disabled family members, recovering from past emotional traumas, etc. But avoiding these discussions early in the process does nothing to lessen the blow later.

Use wisdom to be honest about your situation in a timely fashion.

At the same time, love is an intricate part of your communication. Because of some of the issues you may have contended with, there may be some boundaries you require to first feel safe in the relationship. Communicate those boundaries. Love can be direct, firm, and vulnerable all at the same time. Sharing your needs is not just demanding... it's required. When you communicate with love, it's to the advantage of both parties, not just you. Ultimately, truth is sexy. Truth is vulnerable. Truth is transparent. But above all else, truth is love.

It took a lot for me to feel safe sharing the nitty-gritty details of my past with Samantha. It wasn't easy and felt very risky. For all I knew, she could have walked away at any time. If you don't feel safe telling the truth about your past, your personality, or your quirks to the person you're interested in, let them know that you still have things you need to keep private. But don't massage the truth. Don't put on a show. Most importantly, don't lie. Remember, it's hard to regain trust that has been broken.

If you've lied to someone you're involved with, don't spend another day torturing yourself with the shame, guilt, and fear rolling around inside you. No matter how afraid you are that they'll reject or abandon you, clear the air without excuses. (The only exception to this is if you have reason to believe that telling the truth will endanger you physically. If this is the case, you might consider seeking professional help.)

As we began opening up during our long conversations, we discovered issues that we had to confront. For instance, I realized that I didn't know how to fight fair. Through all my destructive relationships, I had picked up some truly awful habits. My first wife and I were in constant conflict. Even when we weren't arguing, there was static in the room. Not only did we not fight fair, we actively looked for any and every opportunity to kick each other when we were down. My wife was a skilled technician in verbal slice and dice. My own weapons of choice were loud rants, intimidation, and disappearing acts.

One of the ways I overcame this was by asking myself, *What do I really want the end result of this conversation to be?* It's not a matter of being right. It's not a matter of winning. It's a matter of understanding. If two people can keep that question as their focus, they will have discovered the secret to fighting fair.

From the start, Samantha has been my listening ear as I continue to process my relationship issues. She has truly become my safe haven, in every way, and I hers. It's crucial for two partners to be able to say that about each other. I still don't necessarily have it all together, but I do have a person I can talk to, someone I can voice my fears to. She has never discounted any of my concerns or issues. She also never takes these fears personally, becoming defensive or critical.

Becoming a safe haven for someone is one of the most valuable gifts we can offer of ourselves. I learned the value of allowing your partner to express their feelings, even the negative ones (sometimes especially those), without rushing to judgment or trying to fix them. Feelings don't need to be fixed.

Our relationship grew in depth and strength the more we witnessed ourselves committing to personal growth. But between the two of us, we could only go so far. It seemed appropriate for us to explore a third party to take our union to the next level. In the spirit of that, we vowed to undergo a six-month endeavor in premarital counseling. This is when we waded out into the deep end.

During these periods, we were challenged on our core beliefs about money, child-rearing, work, opposite-sex friendships, extended family, roles and responsibilities, faith, and sex. A long list, to be sure, but it's far from exhaustive. This was one of the most important decisions we made in the nurturing of our relationship. We covered an extremely broad range of issues in our sessions, which has made me a big believer in comprehensive counseling. Don't leave anything out. By doing so, you're asking for trouble.

We started out with lists. One for me, and one for Sammy. Individually, we wrote down five things that made us feel loved, and five others that made us feel unloved.. These lists are included on the previous page. Interestingly enough, by the time our first anniversary came around, the items on our lists had changed substantially. We had grown. Our relationship had matured as trust and security was more firmly developed. The things that had affected us in the beginning were no longer issues.

When we started, Sam felt unloved by sarcasm. I felt unloved for not being treated with respect. But after a year of marriage, I found myself naturally refraining from sarcasm. On the other side, Sam had seen me grow in so many areas that showing me respect became as natural as breathing.

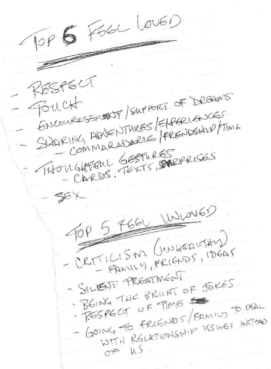

Figure 1: Angus' List

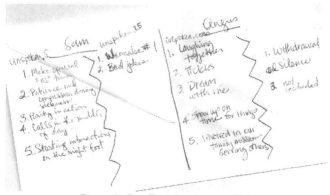

Figure 2: Our First Anniversary Lists

Since the old lists were now irrelevant, we made new ones, right there at the table of the restaurant, at our anniversary dinner. We jotted them down on the back of the envelope of the card I had gotten her for the occasion. The funny thing was that neither of us could come up with more than two things that made us feel unloved. Now that's progress! We've developed to the point where our first instinct is to look out for the other person's best interests.

If you have a partner, ask them to join you in this. You may be surprised to hear what the other has to say. One thing's for sure: your lists won't match. Place your partner's list on your mirror and look at it every day. If your partner feels loved when you spend time with her, don't buy her a gift and then work all weekend. I know, duh!

CHAPTER TWELVE
Taking the Plunge

As I said before, I had serious retardation in my progress towards love in the first marriage. Some things I was simply ignorant of, while others I could chalk up to severe selfishness. There were many things I ignored and didn't even bother to look at. In my experience with Samantha, I wanted to be more purposeful. What follows are important areas of character I considered before taking the plunge.

This idea of being intentional led us to uncover some specific areas our counselor pressed us to address, both to discover more of ourselves and each other. Sammy and I spent a lot of time on this and I think these are areas everyone should take into account when choosing a life partner.

COMMUNICATION

Yes, this is an often reiterated concept, and no, this won't be too cliché. With Samantha and I, we *had* to talk about so many issues as our relationship developed. Our talks were open, candid, and lengthy more times than not. Truth be told, none of the following would have even transpired had we not been able to create a sense of safety and trust between us. That took a lot of patience and hard work.

There is, however, no silver bullet here on how to accomplish this. Every couple is different, so it's crucial that two people endeavor to figure out what works for them. For us, using terms like "I feel" helped tremendously: "When you do this, I feel like you aren't really listening." "Last night, I left feeling..." or "That sarcasm really makes me feel disrespected."

What I found was that the most important part in our communication was when I became an active listener. I asked questions instead of judging, and found myself actually listening from her perspective. In other words, I shut my mouth and put myself in her shoes. If there was conflict, it help me to understand what I had done, perhaps inadvertently, to hurt or offend her.

The more the two of us talked and worked out our differences, the less we took offenses personally. I started to believe that Sammy actually had my best interest in mind and that she wasn't just trying to mess with my heart. That was *huge*! It inspired me, made me feel connected, and caused me to open up myself to be even more vulnerable.

This was so challenging for both of us. We'd both been hurt, we'd both been abused, and we both knew we had to push through that junk if we were ever going to find peace. As difficult as it can be, solid communication is so worth t!

MONEY

There's an old proverb that states, "Where your treasure is, there also is your heart." Someone who frivolously spends money on extravagances often reveals compensated insecurities, whereas another person may routinely give to non-profit organizations, displaying generosity. These are just two examples, but obviously the list of potential financial allegiances is very long.

For Sammy and I, we both share a generous approach towards supporting causes and organizations we believe in. We are both strong proponents of social justice. Easy!

However, where we struggled was in what we put aside for the future. We had found our biggest strains in trying to establish a B-U-D-G-E-T. This word had never entered our vocabulary before. We always spent money on whatever we wanted, whenever we wanted it. Both of us lived paycheck to paycheck.

Then our counselor introduced us to Dave Ramsey. He really pissed us off at first with his "restrictions," as we perceived them. Yet our plans for children and a future demanded a different approach. Would you believe that within our first year of marriage, we were saving money, agreed on supporting specific charities, bought a car with cash, had a rainy day fund, and paid off all of our credit cards?

Money is such a big part of our lives, and how we spend it can reveal our priorities. Some invest their assets, short-term or long. They're already thinking about the future, about security, about provision. Others go belly up if they miss the next paycheck. Some have a closet full of lovely new clothes which can send a message of style and flair, but don't miss the fact that another totally different message may underlie that cool and hip veneer.

Do I want to be with someone who feels compelled to keep up with all the latest electronic toys and gadgets? How about the fella with a brand new truck every year or the girl with more frequent flyer miles to vacation destinations than that Amazing Race host?

Some call these people "high maintenance."

Don't misunderstand me. Having money is totally fine, even necessary. But I think great amounts of character are evidenced through *how* a pocketbook is used.

BEING WRONG

Another strong barometer of character we observed is how a person handles being wrong. Let's face it, most of us don't like being wrong... but it's bound to happen. Perhaps it happens to some people more often than others, but at some point or another, everybody finds themselves in the unenviable position of being wrong. Just plain wrong. It's something we all have to deal with.

I've been around people who never take ownership of their inherent wrongness. Instead, they steer themselves into denial or, worse, blame. Some people are just psychologically incapable of admitting fault, and though it may show up in the beginning of the relationship as something to joke about, it will only get more and more difficult to live with.

For me, in the past, I would always swing into a defensive posture and attack back. I thought that if I barraged the perceived enemy with verbal assaults, that would somehow deflect the focus from my own fault. Yet, as I developed and matured, I learned how to laugh and not take myself so seriously. Best of all, I even learned how to agree with someone and admit, "Yup, I was totally wrong!"

I've sat through a lot of counseling sessions, on both sides of the table, and have come to the realization that this is one of the greatest hurdles to a person's growth. Will they own their faults and recognize when they're wrong? Until they come to this critical point, they live in a charade that isolates them from having to face the prospect of losing an argument. How easy it is for them to get trapped in a victim mentality, always blaming circumstances, people, and the past for current chaos. You might ask how I know this. Well, what can I say except that it takes one to know one?

A person of character accepts their own fault. In fact, a person of integrity will acknowledge being wrong without confrontation. This is a person I'm trying to become more like everyday.

OFFENSE

Me and Sammy's long interrogations led to conflict, without a doubt, and where there's conflict, there's the potential for offense. How a person deals with offense is another important question to ask yourself. Allowing yourself to enter conflict with your partner can be very healthy and will give you the opportunity to answer that question definitively.

I had obviously grown in this area a great deal. However, witnessing my soon-to-be wife handle conflict with poise, patience, and reflection totally inspired me. She caused me to question myself about why I felt as I did or how I arrived at my opinions. Questions seemed to stir greater communication than accusation.

Some people can get frustrated, defiant, argumentative, or even take a swing at you. Or perhaps they go the other direction, becoming dismissive, withdrawn, or pouty. Any of these reactions reveal the real person. Whatever the thorny issue is, religious or political or something entirely different, an unwavering front is not something to be greatly desire

I've witnessed a person take issue with me so deeply that our friendship turned suddenly antagonistic. Just how deeply does a person take an argument personally when they're offended? Offense can cause a person to strike back with vile words or actions for no reason other than that they don't agree. Believe it or not, there are a lot of people out there who demand complete agreement as a prerequisite for even basic friendships.

The older I get, the less I need to be right or have all the answers. I recognize that there are a lot of questions out there that are, quite appropriately, over my head. Instead of finding this unsettling, it turns out to be comforting sometimes. That may not have been true ten years ago, but these days, I'm quite comfortable to answer tough questions with three simple, freeing words: "I don't know." Try it sometime.

EMBARRASSMENT

This is one area where Sammy and I had much in common. We both tend to laugh at ourselves more often than not—even to the degree of humoring others through our self-deprecating experiences.

What does your partner do when they're embarrassed? This is another question that may seem unimportant on the surface, but if you think about it, it's a question you'd probably really like to have answered. It has been said that the size of a person's ego is revealed at the height of embarrassment. This is far truer than most people realize.

Personally, when I face embarrassment, I prefer to get giddy. It may not save face, but at the end of the day, it's nice not to have that kind of pressure. Perfection, after all, is pretty hard to maintain, so when the veneer is cracked, what you see underneath is nothing but the ugly truth. When people get angry or enraged, you're invited to a display of their ego at its worst.

Our actions don't have to define us; neither do our embarrassments.

FORGIVENESS

Have you ever noticed that everybody wants to be forgiven when they're in the wrong, but a large number of us simply refuse to forgive others? Of course you have. What a sad state of affairs we find ourselves in. From a psychological perspective, many of us don't even forgive ourselves for things that happened deep in our past. We project that unforgiveness onto others, usually without thinking about what we're doing. The effects can be disastrous.

Here's the reasoning: why should I forgive you if I can't even forgive myself? You can see the true nature of a person's heart when they choose to withhold forgiveness.

As I stated earlier, scorekeeping is truly debilitating. Sammy and I were not about to allow that into our relationship.

WORLDVIEW

This last one is a little more complicated. Our counselor was brilliant in helping us comprehend how our families, our pasts, and our experiences contributed to our filters of the world around us.

What influences your value system and decision making?

I'm definitely not an expert in this area, but I do recognize that a person's worldview is everything. However, what goes into the creation of a worldview is debatable. Some would say you're born with certain tendencies and traits. Others would say that you're a product of your environment and experiences. I tend to think the reality is a bit more complicated than that, that it's all of the above mixed with choices you make along the way. If that's true, our worldview is flexible, not rigid as some believe. As with all things, change is possible—even recommended much of the time. But if your worldview is amendable and capable of further development, you need to ask yourself a simple question: What establishes your worldview?

To begin with, your sense of morality makes up the lion's share of your worldview. Morality seems to be subjective, depending on our current environment. Therefore, some cultures are open to skirts, cleavage, and spatula-applied makeup, whereas some Middle Eastern cultures might frown upon such gross excess. There's no way around it. Culture plays a huge part in the equation, and therefore a huge part of worldview.

So what determines how you treat your neighbor, if you get involved in the PTA, or if you serve at the local soup kitchen? What is it that drives or compels you to protest a poor political decision? What basis do you have for the way you see yourself? Is your form of personal measurement the glamour of television, Muscle & Fitness, the Koran, Grandpa's sage advice, Sunday school, the Joneses, or what was modeled for you in high school? Something sets your roots, is your point of reference, and dictates your moral compass.

In the same fashion, you want to learn the basis of your partner's influences. Are they compatible with yours? Are they contradictory? This is one of the most important areas the two of you need to establish for yourselves. It determines your expectations in politics, faith, education, generosity, and so much more. If you have different worldviews, one or both of you may need to compromise, which if done reluctantly can leave fractures at the foundation of your relationship. Discovering this will greatly dictate whether or not you and your mate will make it.

CHAPTER THIRTEEN
Celebrations

In a time when family connections are increasingly viewed as being more burdensome than warm and nurturing, I treasure them all the more... which is why I started to feel a strong push to introduce Samantha to my family. Because I was spending so much time with her, I wanted her to meet the Nelson clan. I wanted her to become more than my partner in life; I wanted her to be a part of my family. I had been talking her up in every conversation with my parents for months by then, and it was clear that they were intrigued with this Sammy they'd heard so much about.

Finally, the time was right. For Thanksgiving, Samantha and her daughter accompanied me up to Wisconsin to meet everyone. My desire was for my family to fall in love with the two of them as much as I had. It turned out to be an easy sell. Everybody loved them in a heartbeat, so much so that just before we left at the end of the week, my mum was already offering me one of her rings for any "future engagements." It wasn't a particularly subtle hint.

Of course, I'd already made the decision to ask her to marry me. To that end, I had ordered a ring of my own, but I kept quiet about it. As much as I come down on secret-keeping between couples, this was one secret I felt justified in keeping to myself. This was going to be a surprise of epic proportions.

The week I got back, I spoke to her father and requested permission to ask her hand in marriage. I guess I'm just an old-fashioned guy, but that's one tradition I have a lot of respect for. He gave his blessing.

For Christmas, the three of us headed to New York City to meet her side of the family. In sheer numbers, she had me beat. I had a lot of names to remember during that trip. We arrived on Saturday, December 23, and went immediately downtown to see a Broadway play with Samantha's sister and her husband. *Beauty and the Beast* was playing, with Donny Osmond in the part of Gaston. This was my first Broadway show, and it was magnificent. We had box seats, from which we could see every detail of the performance. I was in heaven!

Afterwards, the group of us bustled down to Times Square for dinner, and from there to Rockefeller Center to ice skate under the famous Christmas tree. We had to stand in line over an hour to get onto the rink, but it was well worth the wait. The tree was lit up and thousands of people glided about on the ice. The city lights illuminated the sky around us. It was a magical evening, not to mention warm; at 53 degrees, it was positively balmy for a winter night in New York.

Over the past few weeks, Samantha and I had been regularly discussing the subject of merging two lives into one. As we skated, I brought it up again. To her, it may have seemed like just another in a series of conversations, but for me it was all part of the set-up. I slowly began to position us in the middle of the rink, biding my time for the perfect moment to make my move.

Then, rather suddenly, I got down on one knee and asked Samantha Bernadel to marry me.

At first, she was taken aback, eyes welling up with tears. As I waited for the full meaning of that singular moment to fully settle into place, the skaters around us stopped what they were doing to watch. Pretty soon, they broke into applause and began cheering us on. Thousands of complete strangers stood witness to this, the ultimate expression of our romance, as if that was what they had gathered to be a part of in the first place.

I could sense Sammy's heart pounding. Her mind ran off and she struggled to focus. Normally she was as deliberate and confident a person as I had ever known, but that night under the Rockefeller tree, I saw my future wife completely and utterly flustered. And I loved every moment of it!

As she stood, frozen in time, I quietly whispered to her, "This is the part where you take your glove off." Just like that, the glove came off and I slipped the ring onto her finger. She bent down and emphatically whispered one word into my ear that changed my life forever: "Yes!"

Even though there were people watching us from every angle, I managed to shut out the rest of the world. I was unaware of anybody else around. I was caught up in the two of us, together, and that was it. We kissed, we cried, and we skated in a circle for a bit, until she suddenly stopped and snapped back to reality. She began suspiciously eyeing her sister. "All right, who was in on this?" she asked as we all broke into smiles.

It was far and away the most surreal moment of my life so far.

●●✦●●

As is usually the case, wedding considerations became an immediate priority. Since we had both been through prior marriages, we didn't want to blow a ton of money this time around. That said, we also knew we didn't want to hold a single day of festivities only to disappear from all the beloved family and friends who had traveled so far to celebrate with us. We managed to meet both of those criteria.

Because the lease on my apartment was going to expire very shortly, it became advantageous for us to hold a "legal" wedding before a "family" wedding could be arranged. With an 11-year-old daughter in the house, we wanted to model to her the importance of making a marriage commitment. After our six months of premarital counseling, we settled on an extremely small wedding ceremony with just close friends. Including a photographer and my good friend and mentor Bruce to officiate, there were only nine of us in attendance.

We met at my apartment on the afternoon of July 7, 2007 (yes, that's 07/07/07). There was a long peninsula extending into the lake that my apartment community was nestled along, and at the end of it stood a spectacular weeping willow whose canopy spread from one extreme of the small grassy island to the other. This beautiful setting served as a background to our special day.

It was cloudy, rainy, and cool that morning, and even throughout the afternoon, but we were determined to stand outside in the rain if the weather wasn't going to cooperate with our plans. Fortunately, our perseverance paid off. Right at 4:00, the clouds broke and a gorgeous yellow haze filled the air. We all scurried down the path toward the willow tree only to find, to our amazement, that a host of ducks and geese had converged on the same spot—seemingly to witness the occasion. As we looked up at the streams of sunlight coming down through the light clouds, it was clear that God's lighting technicians had orchestrated a perfect moment just for us.

The ceremony that followed was simple, short, and relaxed. With so few people with us, we experienced the power of true intimacy. Afterward, we headed out to celebrate in style at Ruth's Chris Steakhouse.

This event, of course, was only the teaser for what was to come. We still had three months to plan the family wedding. On the advice of a friend, we located an area just six hours away, along the Gulf coast outside of Panama City Beach, Florida.

Carillon was a gated community located right on the beach and offered a great selection of gorgeous rental homes. We decided to rent one of the houses for an entire week and have our family join us there.

What mattered most was that we wanted to have our ceremony on the beach. We weren't picturing it as being a celebration of just the two of us, Sam and Angus, but as a celebration of the whole group, the process of two families becoming one. It was a beautiful intertwining.

Upon our arrival, we checked into the rental, which was much larger and grander than we had expected. There was an open format kitchen, living, and dining area with a large table that was able to accommodate the entire group—a fantastic feature for meals, socializing, and raucous Canasta matches (or, as we call it in my family, Ca-*nasty*).

There was a pool in the backyard, a barbecue grill, granite countertops, a flat-screen TV, and killer sound system with speakers installed throughout the entire house. For the whole week, we were living in the lap of luxury.

Throughout that first day, family and friends trickled in, cell phones ringing with each arrival. The celebration had begun. In the evening, the beach house was buzzing with activity, introductions, laughter, and love. It wasn't until very late in the night that we all wandered off to sleep, even though the actual wedding was to be held the next day.

In the morning, the ladies headed out for pedicures while the men converged on a par-three golf course just down the road. It seemed pointless to play at one of the more spectacular nearby courses when the majority of our party sucked at golf. The outing itself was less about clubs, swings, and score than it was about trash talk and peacock strutting. It was male bonding at its finest.

After a quick lunch, we all scattered to get dressed. By this time, my excitement was at a fervor. Once everyone had reassembled, the party walked leisurely through the lovely streets toward the beach. The guests went ahead of us to sprinkle rose petals in the sand. The time had come.

Everyone was in position as Sam's daddy drove her up in the rental van. The two of them strolled down the pier stairs arm-in-arm. Our daughter had created a large heart-shaped impression in the sand, and we stood in the middle. At this point, my father, who's also a pastor, stepped forward and spoke for a few minutes, his words peppered with affirmation and well-timed humor. Afterwards, Bruce spoke up and shared some of his own observations of our growth as a couple. Together, everyone united around us as Sam's daddy blessed us with compassionate, tear-filled words as we all prayed.

It's difficult for me to express how powerful that moment was. It was intimate, romantic, and family focused. It was beyond words, impossible to convey. It was extraordinary.

We had timed the ceremony to end just as the sun was beginning to set. Cameras began clicking away furiously, trying to capture the picturesque beauty of those final moments out on the beach. My bride was radiant. Once again, the perfection of God's lighting technicians took my breath away.

From there, we went out for dinner and toasts at an English-style pub on the beachfront called the Boar's Head. We feasted on prime rib, pecan-encrusted halibut, and barbeque ribs. Everyone was having an incredible time. The cake was cut, the champagne corks popped, and the toasts—not to mention a few tears—flowed freely. Sammy and I wore our hearts on our sleeves as we humbly and emotionally expressed our appreciation and love for those who were most important to us. In particular, we spoke highly of our parents, for it was not without recognition that the two of us had turned out to be the sum total of their unconditional love and support, even through our darkest days.

The days that followed were all about family, even for those who weren't blood-related. We enjoyed great food, reminiscing, and lots of late-night Canasty! We hung out at the beach, played by the pool, and invaded the local outlet stores. We even explored the touristy offerings of neighboring Rosemary Beach, Seaside, and Panama City, including dolphin-watching and oyster-shucking.

When the week was over, we had all experienced an incredible time. But most important of all, we had experienced it together. This was what we both felt weddings should be about. We managed to stay under budget, the whole thing costing less than $6,000. Most weddings cost twice that much and aren't half as exhilarating. Believe it or not, people will talk about the fun and frolic they had at a wedding a lot longer than they'll be talking about the chairs, table settings, and floral spreads. There are so many more practical expenditures in married life, it just doesn't make sense to break the bank on day one. Take my advice and save yourself a headache: keep it easy, fun, and family-focused. Celebrate one another, not just the marriage.

I am so psyched that I'm out of the dating business. Except for my wife, that is. When I look back at the need I had when I entered my first marriage, the need to find someone I could share myself with completely, openly, and honestly, I see that it wasn't truly fulfilled. In that marriage, I was always hiding myself, keeping secrets, and walking on eggshells, completely distracted from the things that really mattered.

In marriage, there should be safety, and with my ex-wife there was none, for either of us. To be fair, I was to blame on most accounts. We were both too immature and selfish to recognize what was necessary for a relationship to work, but I was thirty-two years old and should have known better. When I finally met Samantha, all those needs had been contended with and were well on their way to coming to fulfillment. I'm confident in myself and have a strong sense of personal identity. I know who I am, and so does she. We're not "two halves making a whole, but two wholes making a marriage." Between us, we have a relationship that is playful, fun, and ever-growing.

When we first began this book together, I invited you into the darkest days of my life. It was there that I muttered the words, "I need to feel loved," having no idea what that love truly looked like. The reality was that I needed to feel love for myself. But even more importantly, I needed to know the source from which all love comes from before I could ever truly experience the fullness of love with another person.

Through the course of these pages, I found what I had been looking for all of my life, even though it didn't come in the way I had imagined. Despite the fact that I had lost my way and made horrible mistakes, I eventually found direction in my journey for love. It can happen for you, too. I don't care if you've been through dozens of relationships or divorced your high school sweetheart—there is hope for you. Even if you're in a relationship right now that seems hopeless, you can personally experience a transformation of your heart and life.

No matter what your situation, the following chapter will unveil to you the source of love I discovered, the compass that gave me direction. I believe this is what completely turned my life around and will turn your life around as well. The next chapter, though the final one in this story, will hopefully play a part in the opening chapters of your own love story. You *can*, and I believe you *will*, find the love of your life!

CHAPTER FOURTEEN

The Compass

No one told me how messed up my heart could get. There's no health class in high school to prepare you for it, no textbook to lay it out in black and white, no wise professor to pull you aside and say, "The things you do and the decisions you make may not always have a profound effect on your life today, but they will undoubtedly affect your heart immeasurably." I didn't know that my shame and guilt could dramatically destroy my potential. I had no idea that my self-worth, quality of relationships, and passion for life could be so complicated by my actions.

My heart is the real me! It's who I am both to myself and the world around me... and I had grossly abused it. My shame, filth, and brokenness caused me to hide—emotionally, spiritually, and sometimes even physically. I sought refuge in shadows, desperate to avoid bringing any of my "stuff" into the light of day. I couldn't confront my shame. In fact, most of the time I couldn't even admit I had any!

As I stated earlier, I've never been more motivated to experience personal transformation than I was in the wake of my broken marriage. Now, I don't know many people that haven't spent at least some time in prayer when their relationships tanked, even people who aren't overtly spiritual—for that matter, even people who may be antagonistic toward spirituality. At certain desperate moments, people pray. Prayer is as close to universal as anything gets. Granted, most of these prayers are pretty self-indulgent: "Lord, please change my husband/wife" or "God, make this situation go away." I definitely prayed a few of these in my attempts to ease my deep pain and confusion.

Crises draw out yearnings in us for the supernatural. If you're not particularly religious, here's the thing: the solution that completely changed my life wasn't based in religion. That's all too ironic for a fella who at one point held a perfect pedigree as a Christian. As it turns out, the answer wasn't theological extrapolation, but rather practical and tangible expression. And truth be told, it's actually something of a paradox.

There are many paradoxes in life. A seed has to die before it grows. Roses are pruned before they flourish. A person has to give in order to receive. Here's a few words about paradox that drives the point home:

> The paradox of our time in history is that we have taller buildings but shorter tempers, wider freeways, but narrower viewpoints. We spend more, but have less; we buy more, but enjoy less. We have bigger houses and smaller families, more conveniences, but less time. We have more degrees but less sense, more knowledge, but less judgment, more experts, yet more problems, more medicine, but less wellness.

We drink too much, smoke too much, spend too recklessly, laugh too little, drive too fast, get too angry, stay up too late, get up too tired, read too little, watch TV too much, and pray too seldom. We have multiplied our possessions, but reduced our values. We talk too much, love too seldom, and hate too often.

We've learned how to make a living, but not a life. We've added years to life not life to years. We've been all the way to the moon and back, but have trouble crossing the street to meet a new neighbor. We conquered outer space but not inner space. We've done larger things, but not better things.

We've cleaned up the air, but polluted the soul. We've conquered the atom, but not our prejudice. We write more, but learn less. We plan more, but accomplish less. We've learned to rush, but not to wait. We build more computers to hold more information, to produce more copies than ever, but we communicate less and less.

These are the times of fast foods and slow digestion, big men and small character, steep profits and shallow relationships. These are the days of two incomes but more divorce, fancier houses, but broken homes. These are days of quick trips, disposable diapers, throwaway morality, one night stands, overweight bodies, and pills that do everything from cheer, to quiet, to kill. It is a time when there is much in the showroom window and nothing in the stockroom.[1]

---

[1] Dr. Bob Moorehead is the former pastor of Seattle's Overlake Christian Church. He retired in 1998 after 29 years in that post. The essay appeared in Words Aptly

Each of us is where we are today because of the choices we've made—choices which have often pretty much sucked. I was selfish, arrogant, and thickheaded. Stupid even. What an intensely difficult revelation this was! I could not, despite my best efforts, change ME.

My life perpetuated a cycle of self-defeat each time I attempted to course correct. I was insane, and I absolutely mean that. If it's true, as it's been said by many others before me, that insanity means doing the same thing over and over again whilst expecting different results, than I was the poster boy for insanity. What I needed was to do something completely, mind-blowingly different.

I needed to die.

Well, hold on there before pulling that pistol out of your nightstand. I'm not talking about suicidal death. It was a paradoxical death.

There's an old proverb that says, "Though a man dies, yet shall he live." Like, all those artists who dreamt of being famous, only to ironically achieve it through death? No, the kind of death I'm talking about is like "letting go," letting go of my pride, letting go my ego, letting go of my self-perception. This kind of death is highly intentional, painful, and lingers a lot longer than a gunshot, which may seem like a detractor. But letting go actually has much to recommend it. Again, stay with me.

If you were to get just one thing out of this entire book, just one thing, here's what it needs to be:

YOU CAN'T CHANGE YOU.

Spoken, Dr. Moorehead's 1995 collection of prayers, homilies, and monologues used in his sermons and radio broadcasts.

I know what you're thinking. I should have led with that in the first chapter so as to save you some time and energy.

So, you can't change you. What do I mean by that?

Let me explain. You see, I tried the normal prescription for change, which is better nutrition and exercise, going for counseling, trying to quit habits, and attending church. That's what people do when they need to change. In fact, all of these things are positive and helpful... but only in the short-term. If you do all that, you've probably just embarked on a comprehensive regimen of behavioral modification. Remember that list in Chapter 8? Those were good modifications, but they were still behavioral. I was still the same person underneath it all. Very little internal change had occurred. For example, I tried to quit smoking a gazillion times. One time, I even went back, late at night, and dug out a pack I'd trashed from a gas station garbage can. Pretty pathetic. The point is, each time I failed, I bought my next pack and felt more defeated than ever.

Somehow, in the midst of my struggle for change, I started to see my heart as a compass. It's a truly useful analogy. On the compass, due north is established by my choices, experiences, and environments. The needle of a compass will always, always, always point towards due north.

A while ago, I read something that struck me as profound: "We are today what we've continually thought ourselves to be." At some time or another, I placed false beliefs in my heart about who I was. I thought, on some level, that I didn't deserve to be happy. I had crossed an invisible line along the way that disqualified me from experiencing hope and fulfillment. I had screwed up too much. I thought I needed to be punished for indulging in pornography, living without character, and cheating on my wife... for being a manwhore.

Unfortunately, whatever your heart has been connected to determines your natural and effortless responses in life, the due north. When I used behavior modification to "change" myself, it was like grabbing the needle of my heart's compass and twisting it around with nothing more than willpower and determination. This kind of change demands that you never loosen your grip on the needle, because as long as you're still the same person beneath the surface the needle is going to automatically snap back to due north. That's why the normal prescriptions for change are only helpful in the short-term. The moment I grew fatigued, I let go of the needle and it snapped back, returning me to my old coping mechanisms.

Since this was a repetitive cycle, forcing and releasing the needle, I needed a new approach to change. I had to redirect my heart's natural responses. I had to change "due north." This was a daunting task. Imagine the force required to turn the world on its axis, to literally change the polarity of north and south. There was only one way for me to radically and permanently alter my life's direction. I had to go to the roots of my behavior in the deepest recesses of my heart.

It seems to me that each and every one of us has a spiritual nature, however we choose to define that. Christianity, as I've heard it taught, tells us that we, as human beings, are made up of three distinct but complementary parts: body, soul, and spirit. In this model, the body is our physical being. The soul is comprised of our mind, will, and emotions. The spirit, on the other hand, is somewhat harder to define. It's the element of our nature that gives us purpose and direction. It is the breath of life within us. But mysteriously missing from this list is the heart. Where does the heart enter into the picture? If I were to take a guess at it, I think it's a combination of the spirit and soul realms, directly connecting our thoughts and emotions to our identity. An old Jewish Proverb states, "Guard your heart, for out of it flows the issues of life."

I got to a point where I had to put aside all my filters and doctrinal understandings, everything I had been taught to believe and learned since I was a boy. Doctrine hadn't helped thus far. It only seemed to make me more argumentative, arrogant, and right—almost as if I had become a Pharisee of legalism, not love. In fact, if you look at world history, it's nothing short of ironic that religious bias is the cause of more harm and pain than any other abuse known to history. When I operate out of a religious mindset, I notice how I become condemning, critical, judgmental, and can easily leave God and His nature out of the equation. Religion is performance-based... and I've had enough of performance. I wanted less of the organization and more of the Organizer.

It appeared to me that a relationship *with* God, not *about* God, seemed to be a more appropriate response to my Creator. God, known and experienced, is life, joy, peace, and vitality. And like any relationship, we imitate those with whom we associate.

I had a desire within me to believe that I was a part of something bigger than myself. I desperately needed that to be true. At times, you and I even catch glimpses of greatness within ourselves, flows and surges of wisdom and strength, perseverance and brilliance. These moments show up when we least expect them, and they're tremendously encouraging.

With all these concepts and ideas swirling through my head, I began playing around with them. If it was true that I was created in the image of God, which I felt had to be true even after the most tortuous re-evaluation of my doctrinal and theological upbringing, then I came to realize that there were only two possibilities that underlie the entirety of creation. Either God was one screwed-up, schizophrenic being or I was screwed-up and schizophrenic, almost hopelessly so. Given those two options, it was easy to see which one was more plausible. After all, I'm inclined to believe our world is a little too amazing to have been created by any being less than stellarly intelligent. So, I had no choice but to err on the side of my own idiocy. Now *that* I would have no trouble believing in.

On the day we were born, we were given the full capacity to experience and appreciate all that God is: His narrative is our narrative, and it qualifies us for beauty, grace, power, glory, creativity, gentility, kindness, patience, right-standing, mercy, favor, forgiveness, purity, love, honor, and fulfillment. We inherit His nature, His character, His view, and His opinion.

Perhaps you're saying to yourself, "Great. So why don't I feel like that when I get up each morning, huh?" I wouldn't blame you for asking this, since my own question was somewhat similar. I asked, "If that's even remotely possible, could someone please explain to me how I've traded all that goodness for what I'm experiencing, this facsimile, in effect this lie that I live in today?" Well, that's a big question. Unfortunately, I'm not necessarily smart enough to answer it—I don't have any degrees. The only thing I could muster in response to myself was my own experience.

Now, remember what I said before: you can't change you. But there's a catch.

YOU'RE NOT WHO YOU THINK YOU ARE!

Instead of walking in who you really are, the you that doesn't need to change, you've believed you are the person you see yourself to be. You've looked into the mirror, seen the facsimile, the lie, and believed it without question. And the lie comes from you. You are an actor writing your own script as you go, ad-libbing every line. Whether through your own mistakes, your upbringing, or your choices, you see yourself in light of your own performance. You allow the past to dictate your being. Like me, this system of thinking, of failure, flooded your thought life and imagination, hindering your ability to reach your own potential to be who you really are. It doesn't matter if you've had fourteen failed relationships, or even a hundred. I failed so many times, I started to hate myself. Your failures, however, do not define you, unless you let them. It's no wonder we continue to repeat these vicious cycles, because honestly, if I don't like me, why should anyone else? Why would even God like me? This kind of thinking is like a virus that sweeps in and crashes a computer. So who are you? Who's your true self and where's it been hiding all this time?

To find yourself again, look no further than your heart.

Think about all the times you've tried to save face and maintain the appearance of leading a perfect life. Our culture perpetuates the perceived obligation and expectation to keep the performance going. The show must go on! By doing everything we can to maintain the illusion, to keep the mask from slipping, we completely fail to deal with the root of our hearts, and that's where our deepest hurts get hidden away. We lock them up in the vault and throw away the key. But they never go away, and instead inflict major damage. This psychology causes us to try, to strive, to exert great effort on a continual basis. There is no rest. There is no relief. We don't know that our false belief systems are crippling us, delivering knockout punches where we're the most vulnerable.

I was dying and didn't even know it.

The further I walked along this path of discovery, the more I connected with some powerful, healing truths:

1. I am not the sum total of my past experiences.
2. I am not the labels placed upon me.
3. I am not the weight of my pain.

All I was striving for, all I was exerting that great effort for, was to achieve beauty, acceptance, confidence, and security. Except that all of those things were already inside me, placed there at the moment I came into the world. Living inside me was everything I ever wanted, dreamed, or desired for myself. It was encoded as a birthright into the real me, into my heart.

Here's my understanding: in the beginning, God created the first man, Adam, a creation in the full and complete image of God Himself. Adam fell according to his performance, thus dooming all of mankind to the same fate. From that point forward, we were not living in the reality of who we were in God, or experiencing the benefits thereof. Therefore, many years later, a second Adam, whose performance *was* perfect, came into the world to restore what the first Adam lost for us all. With that restoration came our ability to once again live in the experience of our God-given identity. Now all the benefits that come with that experience are ours regardless of performance. This "Second Adam" was named Jesus.

I believe that God has placed within me the capacity to live beyond my own experience, education, earning potential, or expectation. Jesus made a way for me to be the person I was always intended to be. The best part is that being my true self and laying claim to my identity is effortless.

I began to learn how to access the resources that were already within me by connecting my reality to God's reality, which was a lot better than the one I had imagined for myself. Making this divine connection took some time for no other reason than I, like most of us, had invested years convincing myself otherwise. Talk about wasted time!

How does transformation happen? You can't walk in happiness until you see yourself happy, you can't walk in love until you see yourself lovable, and you can't walk in peace until you see yourself peaceful. We have to meditate and rehearse what God says about us to such a degree that we *actually see* ourselves in light of those truths. Only then can you experience what you're seeing. That's the transformative power of God for you.

My problems were heart issues, not intellectual ones. Here's the paradox. I didn't change the way I was thinking, I changed the way I believed. In my core, I connected to a new reality, a new perspective. When I strengthened my grip on that viewpoint, transformation happened. Change happened. It just wasn't the kind of change I had started out looking for. The change I found was much better!

On my way to making these realizations, I would go to bed at night often unable to sleep. Instead of lying there dwelling on pain and failure, I chose to change the script. I closed my eyes and imagined a picture in my mind's eye of who I was in light of God's nature. Then I transplanted that vision of myself into a current circumstance. Next, I connected to the emotions that came along with this new imagined reality—peace, relief, shamelessness, and absolutely no guilt whatsoever. When I opened my eyes, having connected His truth to my truth, I discovered it wasn't an imagined reality at all! It was the real thing.

I kept thinking, "You are what you think you are." I dwelled on that until realizing that if my thoughts were based on my own past, my behavior would be limited by it. However, if my thoughts were based on His truths, His abilities, and His unlimited potential, my life could become a reflection of those new beliefs. The realization allowed me to dig myself out of years of repressed hurt and emerge on the other side of it unscathed. Even after being buried under a heap of emotional garbage for years, my true self was just as beautiful and pure as the day I was born.

Our ability to live a fantastic life is our own responsibility, or rather our response to His ability. When we yield our nature to His, when we die to ourselves, everything changes in our self-perception. And not only our self-perception, but also our opportunities and relationships. Confidence, self-worth, and value now become our everyday experience. My life becomes an expression of His love.

I was astounded. "Could it really be that easy?" I asked. "Are you freaking kidding me?" But then, that's part of the lie. We think real, permanent change has to be difficult. Ultimately, it really isn't. It's simply yielding to the real you, the you God made. What could be easier?

When your heart changes, your choices change, your behaviors change… and your relationships change. Make it real, make it permanent, make it effortless. All transformation starts in the heart.

All this time, I was an actor playing a part. In my script, I created the role of a manwhore, and cast myself in it. But I was in the wrong movie entirely. God had written a better role for me, and it had been inside me from the very beginning. It was in my heart.

And I was finally listening to it.

I've now shared, as openly and honestly as I know how, the lessons that transformed my life. Perhaps you're in a place where you're trying to be open and honest in your life.

If this story has resonated within you, maybe you're ready, just like I was. I came to the end of myself: my pride, my ego, and my agenda. I decided it was time to enter this paradox for myself in order to receive all that God had provided for me. I finally took a deep, cleansing breath and said these words:

"Jesus, I can't do this. I can't change, I can't be the man I know I'm supposed to be. I give up. I give you me, all of me. Open my eyes, come into my life, and transform my heart."

To them God willed to make known what are the riches of
the glory of this mystery among the Gentiles: which is
Christ in you, the hope of glory.
–COLOSSIANS 1:27 (NKJV)

THE LAST WORD

Are you tired? Worn out? Burned out on religion?
Come to me. Get away with me and you'll recover
your life. I'll show you how to take a real rest. Walk
with me and work with me—watch how I do it.
Learn the unforced rhythms of grace. I won't lay any-
thing heavy or ill-fitting on you. Keep company with
me and you'll learn to live freely and lightly.
–MATTHEW 11:28-30 (MSG)

My story is far from unique. The struggles and pain I experienced aren't special, but neither was my recovery. You can do it, too! My transformation wasn't a product of aligned stars or Hollywood magic. What happened to me came about as a result of intentionally going after God. What you've read is deeply transparent and vulnerable, a perspective that came only as a result of my experience. I've left nothing out.

In the coming months, I hope that you too will connect to a greater understanding of your need to connect with God's best. Your heart is waiting for you to rediscover it. You can experience right now the overwhelming grace and love that Jesus came to bring in an immeasurably powerful way, and the fact that you're reading this is a confirmation that you are ready to move to the next level.

I want to continue this journey with you through the use of technology. At my website, www.angusnelson.com, you'll find helpful and inspiring resources, most of which are free for you to use, copy, write on your mirror, or quote to your friends.

In the next several months, you may find yourself coming down with a case of the crazies or spiritual schizophrenia. Know that you're not alone. Others have gone before you to help lead the way back to sanity.

Even if things are bleak right now, remember: your best days are yet to come.

ABOUT THE AUTHOR

Angus Nelson lives in Huntsville, Alabama with his wife and three children. His desire to develop leaders and share his faith with others has led him to travel to five continents and twelve countries.

His life has been anything but boring. With a background in theology, he's served as youth leader, worship leader, counselor, speaker, and now, writer. Throughout all this, he's been a waiter, ski resort ticket checker, carpenter, telemarketer, and landscaper. He's hosed chili vats, stuffed wood chips in bags, sold health club memberships, told off Jean-Claude Van Damme, and even helped Bruce Willis call his bookie once.

As a motivational speaker, Angus has ranked in the top 5% of Monster.com's "Make It Count" high school program and is currently available for college, corporate, and conference speaking events.

More Resources:
www.angusnelson.com

Made in the
USA
Monee, IL